*Scott Squillace is a dedicated lawyer, a gay husband, and an expert on the legal opportunities and land mines for same-sex couples. In* Whether to Wed, *he has written a timely, readable, and thorough starting point for gay and lesbian Americans who are thinking about marriage, grappling with the intricacies of conflicting federal and state laws, and building families—meaning, these days, most of us.*

—Jonathan Rauch
Senior Fellow
The Brookings Institution
Author, *Gay Marriage: Why It Is Good for Gays,
Good for Straights, and Good for America*

*This is a rapidly changing area of law and Scott Squillace's book will help members of the LGBT community evaluate whether marriage is the right way to go. It is written with the non-lawyer in mind—but lawyers will also benefit from its wisdom.*

—Joan M. Burda
Attorney at Law
Author, *Estate Planning for Same-Sex Couples*

*I have been part of the struggle for marriage equality since it began. For me, the fight is more than symbolic. After my husband died suddenly, I was treated like a second-class citizen because of DOMA. Yet it did not come as a surprise. I watched my late husband, Gerry Studds, fight against DOMA in the U.S. House of Representatives. The abstract injury he predicted for me was now real. Even the best legal advice and financial planning could not stop the discrimination DOMA inflicted. I'm proud that I was part of the federal court challenges that led to the Supreme Court defeat of DOMA. The Supreme Court decision now means that all legally married same-sex couples will be treated equally under the law. Scott's book does a great job of moving couples through all the legal benefits and responsibilities marriage brings. It is a practical guide for same-sex couples and financial advisors who work with same-sex couples following the defeat of DOMA.*

—Dean Hara is the surviving spouse of Gerry E. Studds, the first openly gay member of Congress. Hara was a plaintiff in *Gill et al. v. Office of Personnel Management,* 682 F.3d 1 (1st Cir. 2012)

Whether to Wed *is the primer every same-sex couple should read, whether they're contemplating marriage, or if they've already tied the knot. Scott Squillace helps us understand the legal, tax and financial consequences of marriage—both the benefits and the challenges—in an objective, organized and easy-to-understand way.*

—John McGowan
Senior Vice President, Northern Trust
National Practice Leader for LGBT and
Non-Traditional Family Practice

Whether to Wed *demystifies the complex laws that apply to same sex couples, providing a timely, straightforward, and comprehensive guide to use as they consider what's best for their personal situations.*

—David Williams
Intuit Chief Tax Officer and
Executive Director of the American Tax and
Financial Center at TurboTax

# WHETHER

*to*

# WED

# WHETHER

## *to*

# WED

## A LEGAL *AND* TAX GUIDE

### *FOR*

## GAY *AND* LESBIAN COUPLES

## SCOTT E. SQUILLACE, Esq.

Foreword by
The Right Reverend Gene Robinson,
IX Bishop of New Hampshire, The Episcopal Church

Squillace & Associates, P.C.
Boston, MA

Published by

Squillace & Associates, P.C.

Boston, MA

Publisher's Cataloging-in-Publication Data

Squillace, Scott E., Esq.

>Whether to wed : a legal and tax guide for gay and lesbian couples / by Scott E. Squillace.—Boston, MA : Squillace & Associates, P.C., 2014.

>p. ; cm.

>ISBN13: 978-0-9860490-0-2

>1. Same-sex marriage—Law and legislation—United States—Popular works. 2. Gay couples—Legal status, laws, etc—United States—Popular works. 3. Lesbian couples—Legal status, laws, etc.—United States—Popular works. 4. Taxation—Law and legislation—United States—Popular works. I. Title.

>KF539.S68 2014

>346.730168—dc23                                    2013918055

FIRST EDITION

Project coordination by Jenkins Group, Inc.

www.BookPublishing.com

*Cover design by Chris Rhoads*

*Interior design by Brooke Camfield*

Printed in the United States of America

18   17   16   15   14  •  5   4   3   2   1

# Dedication

*To my parents, Richard and Elaine Squillace, high school sweethearts still after fifty-five years of marriage. Their model taught me a great deal about what marriage means;*

*And,*

*To Shawn M. Hartman, without whose love and support none of this would have ever been possible.*

# Contents

# Foreword

This is a tumultuous time for LGBT rights in America, particularly when it comes to the debate over same-sex marriage. Religion has and will likely continue to play a significant role in this debate. The concepts of religion and marriage have become inextricably linked in the United States and in other parts of the world. The vast majority of American wedding ceremonies occur in a religious setting, whether in a church, synagogue, or other house of worship; it's difficult to conceive of marriage as separate and distinct from religious practices. What most people fail to remember is that clergy, at the same time as they preside at a religious wedding, are also acting as agents of the state, authorizing civil marriage, even when accomplished in a religious house of worship. (Beneath it all, people do understand this dual role for clergy: If the marriage should end in divorce, the couple doesn't return to the sweet little church where they were married, but rather, they go to the civil courts for a divorce.)

Some religious traditions and expressions, of course, teach that same-sex love is a sin. For those individuals, the idea of same-sex couples participating in a religious practice like marriage can be an affront to their religion. This view, however, ignores the truly dual nature of marriage in the United States. For many people, yes, it is a deeply religious event grounded in their theology. It is a sacrament in the Christian faith, including in the Episcopal Church, where until my recent retirement I served as Bishop of the Diocese of New Hampshire. But it is also a vitally important civic institution. Society determined a very long time ago that marriage benefited the culture by promoting stability, and was therefore worthy of the society's support. In return, the society provides for civil marriage, which brings with it a host of legal rights and responsibilities that can protect one's life partner and children and make a meaningful difference in a couple's life together. At its core, marriage is a promise to care for one another, usually for life.

As a result of this dual nature of marriage—its importance as both a religious and a civil institution—it can, and does, mean different things to different people. Unfortunately, the dual nature of marriage has seriously muddied the debate over whether, and to what extent, the state should recognize same-sex marriages. Many of the arguments against recognition of same-sex marriage state that, because certain religions frown upon same-sex relationships—and by extension same-sex marriage—the state should not recognize it, nor should agents of the state be required to facilitate it. These arguments fail to recognize that marriage, whether of same-sex or opposite sex couples, can exist as a civil construct without infringing on anyone else's religious belief whatsoever. A couple can marry before a justice of the peace or other public official, and will be recognized as married for legal purposes with no religious implications whatsoever; or a couple can marry before an officiant of their faith, and be considered married not only in the eyes of the state, but also in the eyes of their faith. How a couple defines their marriage, and the role of religion (if any) in that marriage, is therefore an intensely personal matter. It is not intended as, and should not be viewed as, an affront to the way that any other couple (or, for that matter, to the way that any religious tradition) chooses to define marriage.

This book focuses on marriage as a civil institution. It is intended to help same-sex couples evaluate the rights and responsibilities that come with marriage, particularly in the areas of tax, financial planning and the law, which are relevant to all couples considering marriage. Understanding the legal and tax implications of taking this step is important for all couples. But given the evolving state of the law in our country, and the patchwork quality of its application among the states, these factors are indeed somewhat confusing for same-sex couples depending, at least for now, on where they live.

However, as the author points out, this book is (intentionally) limited in scope. The issues addressed in this book should not be the only reasons why a couple may or may not choose to become married. This book cannot be a substitute for larger questions around love, commitment, and how you and your partner define the role of marriage in your relationship, in your community, and, perhaps, in your own religious tradition. Only you and your partner, perhaps with prayer or spiritual guidance, can decide how you should do that.

This book can be an important resource to any couple contemplating marriage, not to mention the clergy and other professionals who may be offering counsel to them. A couple's discussion of the issues addressed here should be of enormous help in creating a lasting and secure relationship—with benefits not only to the couple, but to the larger community to which they belong.

—The Right Reverend Gene Robinson
IX Bishop of New Hampshire, The Episcopal Church

# Preface

An otherwise ordinary gay couple, John Arthur and James Obergefell, did something extraordinary recently. There was nothing ordinary about Arthur's horrible (and fatal) diagnosis of amyotrophic lateral sclerosis, or ALS (commonly known as "Lou Gehrig's Disease"), nor of their love and desire to be married. What was extraordinary was when and how their marriage happened, and what it meant for them and, perhaps, for many others around the country.

Both men were forty-seven at the time and had been a couple for more than twenty years. They had long viewed themselves as "married" to one another, despite their home state of Ohio's refusal to legally recognize same-sex unions. Though they had considered traveling to another state to be married, they concluded that until their marriage would be official and recognized at home in Ohio, they were not interested. Then two things happened.

The first event was that in 2011, Arthur was diagnosed with ALS. This progressive neurological disorder slowly makes its victims unable to walk, talk, and, ultimately, to breathe. The couple's time together was growing shorter by the minute.

The second event was that on June 26, 2013, the United States Supreme Court issued a landmark ruling that struck down a portion of the Defense of Marriage Act (DOMA), allowing federal rights and benefits to flow to couples "lawfully married."[1] That day, the two men decided it was time to make their union official. Unfortunately, because of Arthur's condition, that was easier said than done.

Already in hospice care and confined to a medical stretcher, Arthur would have difficulty leaving the couple's home, but it might be possible, they decided, if he were flown on a medical transport plane. Tapping into their network of friends and family around the globe, they raised the $12,700 needed to rent a specially-equipped plane and made arrangements to fly to Baltimore. Maryland was chosen as the destination because it was a state where same-sex marriages were permitted, and because only one person was needed to obtain the marriage license.

Obergefell first flew back and forth to Baltimore on July 9, 2013 to obtain the license. On Thursday, July 11, the couple, Arthur's aunt, Paulette Roberts, who had been temporarily ordained for the occasion, a nurse, and two pilots trained in emergency medicine, boarded a Lear jet and headed to Baltimore-Washington International Airport. The plane parked on the tarmac, the pilots stepped off, and Roberts began the seven-and-a-half-minute ceremony, speaking of the great love between the two that had only grown stronger since Arthur's illness. The men exchanged rings and vows and were pronounced lawfully married, then turned around and flew home moments later.

Once in Cincinnati, Arthur and Obergefell's lawyer filed an emergency lawsuit against the state of Ohio, demanding that their marriage be recognized on the impending death certificate that would soon be issued—or the couple would face "irreparable" harm. The judge ruled in their favor, citing two earlier Ohio cases of marriages that could not otherwise have been lawfully performed in Ohio—but that were legal in the state where they occurred. One had to do with first cousins (who were allowed to be married elsewhere) and another of a young couple who were not, under Ohio law, old enough to be married—but who were old enough in the state where the marriage occurred. In short, they won.[2]

Obergefell's reaction said it best: "In our minds, we've always been married, but now I can actually say John's my husband and have a piece of paper, and a Supreme Court ruling, and a federal government that says, 'Yes, he is your husband.'"

Arthur and Obergefell's desire to have the U.S. government officially acknowledge and affirm their relationship is natural. But how natural is it to have to rent a medical private jet to cross state lines just to get married?!

In the wake of the recent Supreme Court decisions about same-sex marriage, there is some confusion. As of the time this book was written (and it may, hopefully, be outdated by the time you read it), fourteen states and the District of Columbia allow same-sex couples to be married (here-inafter, the "recognition" states); thirty-five states still specifically prohibit it (hereinafter, the "non-recognition" states).[3] In these "United" States, gay and lesbian couples are now left with the question of what it means if one lives in a recognition state and moves or travels to a non-recognition state, or simply lives in a non-recognition state, in terms of the status of their marriage.*

Perhaps more complicated are the couples, like Arthur and Obergefell, who live in a non-recognition state, but go to a recognition state to become married, and then return home. Are they still married? Are they married now only for federal law purposes, but not for state law purposes? What if something happens to one or the other of the couple before the state's law changes? Is a couple from Massachusetts (the first state to recognize same-sex marriage) unmarried when they are on vacation, say, in Virginia? Are they re-married when their plane touches down upon their return?

I will attempt to answer these and other questions in *Whether to Wed: A Legal and Tax Guide for Gay and Lesbian Couples*. The purpose of this book is simple: to help couples from around the country, whether in a rec-ognition or non-recognition state, evaluate, from a legal, tax and financial planning perspective whether it makes sense for them to become married, and what rights and benefits they may expect to receive as a result. Since the law is still evolving, I have provided some guidance for helpful, up-to-date resources you can rely upon to stay apprised of these developments. These are available in the web resources provided in Appendix B, and at www.whethertowed.com.

---

* It is important to note that throughout this book, I use the term "recognition" state to mean a state that recognizes the right for same-sex couples to become married in their state; and "non-recognition" means that state does not allow same-sex marriages. Some non-recognition states may, however, recognize same-sex marriage from other states for some or all purposes, while not allowing it to be performed in their own state. For a list of those "hybrid" recognition states see Table A.1 in Appendix A.

I am mindful of the fact that there are many other, perhaps more important, reasons couples may consider marriage, like love and commitment. I leave those to you and your hearts. What I hope to do here is help evaluate the technical legal, tax and financial planning issues that surround marriage, given the complexities of the law as it currently stands (and continues to evolve) in these United States.

# Introduction

On September 1, 2007, I became happily married to my husband, Shawn Hartman. We met during the summer of 2004 in Boston, just after the *Goodridge* decision had become effective in Massachusetts, the first state to legally recognize same-sex marriage. We found ourselves dating in a world where our relationship actually could result in marriage, something neither of us grew up contemplating would ever be possible. Shawn is from conservative and rural south-central Pennsylvania, and I am from a rather traditional Italian-Catholic household in upstate New York. As a result, in some respects, we were maybe more cautious than some about coming together as a married couple. We took our time deciding about this important commitment.

Presumably, many gay and lesbian couples today face the same happy and daunting reality. Indeed, in my private law practice, I have counseled hundreds of couples grappling with this question of "whether to wed." This book is for them, to help, in part, sort through the legal, tax and financial planning issues surrounding this important question. It is particularly for those in non-recognition states who may still be unclear what federal benefit(s) they may get from becoming married when they return home to a state that doesn't yet recognize their same-sex marriage.

This book is also for the many couples around the country who have long since made their commitments to one another, and who have sorted out the host of issues every couple grapples with when combining lives. Questions such as who is to take out the trash, or, more importantly, who pays for what, and how the house should be titled? Yet they remain unmarried, either because their state does not allow same-sex marriage, or because they are unsure whether marriage makes sense, even now that the federal government does recognize it.

## Before Beginning, a Note about Terminology and Scope

Today's broader gay community is typically referred to in social and political contexts as the LGBT (or GLBT) community. This stands for lesbian, gay, bisexual, and transgender people. More recently the letter "Q" has been added at the end of the list to stand for "queer" or "questioning," so you often see the acronym LGBTQ. All people who identify as such have unique and complex social, legal, tax, and financial planning issues, among other things. Advisors often play an important role in helping this community with these issues. Financial firms in particular are directing marketing efforts toward this demographic.[1]

This book principally addresses the issues facing gay men and lesbian women in the context of a committed long-term relationship. Taken together, and for convenience only (not disrespect), I often refer to all of them herein as the gay community, gay relationships, or gay or same-sex marriage. Personally, I don't believe there are such things as "gay marriage" or "straight marriage," only marriage. The focus of this book is on couple and family relationships within the gay community, especially including committed relationships that attempt to benefit from rights historically provided through civil marriage. The book also includes issues related to the gay community having and raising children. Bisexual, transgender, and queer people have many of the same or similar issues, and some very different ones. Some of the issues addressed in this book will be helpful to those in these communities. To the extent I can point that out, I attempt to do so. I have intentionally kept the scope narrower for this initial publication to address issues related to marriage facing the gay community.

## A Critical Inflection Point

The principle of "equal protection under the law" was enshrined in our Constitution by the Fourteenth Amendment, enacted shortly after passage of the Civil Rights Act of 1866. That amendment solidified certain individual rights following the Civil War. Nearly a century later, the Supreme Court applied this principle to begin to dismantle racial discrimination in our country in the famous *Brown v. Board of Education* decision in 1956 that first articulated the principle that "separate but unequal" is not okay. Now, more than a half a century later, that same Supreme Court and other federal and state courts cite these same principles to begin to dismantle discrimination against gay and lesbian Americans as they seek equal protection under the law for equal access to the right of civil marriage. Some have referred to this effort as the "marriage equality" movement.

At the time of publication of this book, communities in the United States and around the world are experiencing dramatic and progressive advances in gay equality. In the United States, for the first time ever, citizens in several states, by popular ballot initiative, advanced equal marriage rights in the November 2012 elections.[2] Those same elections saw President Barack Obama re-elected to his second term of office, after a fairly acrimonious campaign against Republican Governor Mitt Romney. Governor Romney was fiercely opposed to gay marriage from its inception, when he was governor of Massachusetts where it started. President Obama became the first sitting U.S. president to support same-sex marriage when he announced on May 9, 2012 during his campaign for re-election that his views on same-sex marriage had evolved and he was then in favor of it. He did this despite the fact that some of his strategists advised against it during his re-election campaign.[3] This followed a series of judicial and legislative victories (and some defeats) from the prior decade, including Congress' repeal of the longstanding military policy "Don't Ask; Don't Tell."[4]

More recently, the United States Supreme Court closed its 2012–13 term by announcing a landmark decision in the *Windsor*[5] case by holding Section 3 of the Defense of Marriage Act, or DOMA, unconstitutional and opening the floodgates of federal rights and benefits for thousands of same-sex married couples in the U.S. (The Supreme Court also decided the *Perry*[6] case the same day, which had the effect of allowing same-sex marriages to resume in California—the most populous state in the union.) With these decisions and other events of the past decade, the gay community has gained headway socially, electorally, legislatively, and judicially. Some historians believe that these developments for equality of the gay community, including marriage equality, are comparable in certain respects with the country's civil rights movement, and that the marriage equality movement is its next chapter.[7]

But, like all macro-social changes, these things take time. As of this writing, same-sex marriage is "legal" in fourteen recognition states: California, Connecticut, Delaware, Iowa, Maine, Maryland, Massachusetts, Minnesota, New Hampshire, New Jersey*, New York, Rhode Island, Vermont, and Washington, and the District of Columbia. It is also legal in a variety of foreign countries. (See Appendix D for a more detailed account of the effective date of recognition of same-sex marriages in these states, courtesy of Gay and Lesbian Advocates and Defenders, or "GLAD.") As mentioned, there are still thirty-five states that specifically prohibit same-sex marriage (although a few of those recognize out-of-state same sex marriages for some or all purposes). And there is one state (New Mexico) that neither allows, nor prohibits same-sex marriage. It remains unclear whether all federal rights and benefits will extend to same-sex married couples who move to, or live in, one of those thirty-five states, or whether any of those states will recognize out-of-state same-sex marriages even though they don't allow such marriages to take place there. (Oregon is a recent example of the latter, and is what I will call a "hybrid non-recognition" state.) Unless and until the United States Supreme Court settles the question of whether there is a federal constitutional right (perhaps under equal protection or due process guarantees) for same-sex couples to be married, we will continue to have this patchwork effect of laws around the country.

A map of the United States on the next page illustrates the "patchwork" effect of laws now.

---

* On October 18, 2013, the New Jersey Supreme Court[8] cleared the way for same-sex marriages to begin in the Garden State based on a lower court ruling[9] that found it now unconstitutional under that state's equal protection guarantees to deny same-sex couples the right to marry. This was because the federal government will only provide federal rights based on marriage, not civil unions, which New Jersey had fashioned as its solution to providing rights to same-sex couples. This ruling essentially secured equal marriage in New Jersey and is yet another example of the constant changing landscape in this area. This case, in particular, could become the roadmap for challenging other states' similarly discriminatory laws.

# Legal Status for Same-Sex Couples in the United States as of October 2013

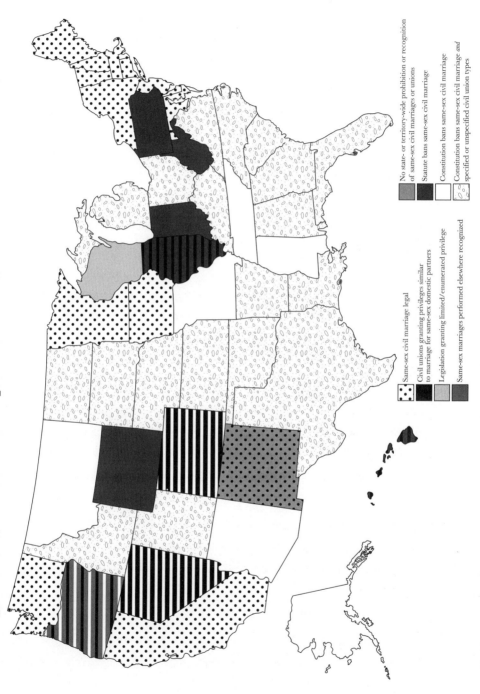

No state- or territory-wide prohibition or recognition of same-sex civil marriages or unions

Statute bans same-sex civil marriage

Constitution bans same-sex civil marriage

Constitution bans same-sex civil marriage *and* specified or unspecified civil union types

Same-sex civil marriage legal

Civil unions granting privileges similar to marriage for same-sex domestic partners

Legislation granting limited/enumerated privilege

Same-sex marriages performed elsewhere recognized

In addition to perhaps being the next iteration of our country's civil rights movement, developments in marriage equality reflect an evolving definition of marriage, much to the chagrin of many conservatives. Shortly after the landmark decision by Massachusetts' highest court in 2003, which found that same-sex couples have a constitutional right to marry (*Goodridge[10]*), there was serious backlash and an immediate attempt to reverse the decision. Governor Mitt Romney (of Massachusetts) and President George W. Bush were both quick to chastise the Justices of the Supreme Judicial Court of Massachusetts as being "activists judges" who were trampling on thousands of years of history of the institution of marriage. Governor Romney admonished: "Beware of activist judges. The legislature is our lawmaking body, and it is the legislature's job to pass laws. . . While the law protects states from being forced to recognize gay marriage, activist state courts could reach a different conclusion, just as ours did. It would be disruptive and confusing to have a patchwork of inconsistent marriage laws between states. Amending the Constitution may be the best and most reliable way to prevent such confusion and preserve the institution of marriage." [11]

President George W. Bush announced a proposal to amend the U.S. Constitution to ban gay marriage, stating, "The reason I did so was because I was worried that activist judges are actually defining the definition of marriage [sic]. And the surest way to protect marriage between a man and woman is to amend the Constitution. . . . I'm deeply concerned that judges are making those decisions, and not the citizenry of the United States." [12]

It only suffices, however, to study the history of the institution of marriage from a legal, social and religious standpoint to realize that it has been anything but static over the centuries. I will briefly review this at the outset of this book to put into context the legal developments we are experiencing. This book is not meant to be a complete exposition on the history of marriage—or even what gay marriage is all about, and why it is good for society. Indeed, that has already been done. [13]

## Overview of the Chapters

Chapter 1 provides a look at the institution of marriage throughout history, including the various iterations of the institution of marriage as it has evolved over the centuries from a social, political, and religious perspective. I also touch on the blurry lines between civil and religious marriage, but point out that in both cases, the institution has evolved and changed and continues to morph in different ways.

Chapter 2 focuses on defining the gay and lesbian community in the United States. I review the demographic information readily available from Census reports and other recognized sources and discuss some of the complexities associated with self-identification and reporting by gay and lesbian people. This chapter also includes a brief overview of the modern gay rights movement, including the critical inflection point of the famous Stonewall Riots in 1969 and how that event led to the movement for equal marriage for gay and lesbian couples.

Chapter 3 tells the story of legal struggles (successes and failures) to recognize, from a legal standpoint, rights of same-sex couples. I also briefly review U.S. statistics of same-sex marriages since it has become lawful, and cite some information about the divorce rate of these marriages. I review the failed early cases on same-sex marriage; discuss the important Hawaii cases in 1993 and 1996 that triggered the debate in Congress which resulted in passing (the now partially defunct) Defense of Marriage Act (DOMA).[14] I then review the history of civil union and domestic partnership legislation and conclude with a discussion of the cases, legislative efforts and ballot initiatives to either pass or outlaw same-sex marriage around the country.

Chapter 4 begins to dive deep into the whether to wed question by explaining in detail the many federal rights and benefits same-sex married couples are now entitled to, as well as pointing out some of the disadvantages and obligations of being married, from a federal law perspective.

Where Chapter 4 covered federal benefits available to same-sex married couples, Chapter 5 continues the whether to wed analysis by delineating the pros and cons of marriage from a state law perspective.

Chapter 6 helps the reader understand the current complexities same-sex couples face as they move (or even travel) around the United States from a state that recognizes their marriage to one that does not. This chapter helps clarify which federal rights and benefits are available to lawfully-married, same-sex couples when they return home to a less friendly state where their marriage is not recognized. For this discussion, I will review, at a very high level, the categories of federal rights and benefits that are affected by where you live (or die), as opposed to simply where you were married. This is referred to as either "place of domicile" rights versus "place of celebration" rights. I will also discuss the hybrid non-recognition states that, while not allowing same-sex marriage in their own state, recognize it if performed in other states.

Chapter 7 then outlines many of the issues for children and families in the context of same-sex couple parenting and, in particular, the issues that arise when those parents get married. Adoption, surrogacy, and custody issues, and how they may factor into the whether to wed decision are broadly discussed.

Chapter 8 is intended to help couples and their advisors evaluate the legal, tax, and financial planning considerations for entering into civil marriage with a particular emphasis on estate planning. It will examine this both from perspectives of living (and dying) in a recognition state versus a non-recognition state.

Chapter 9 takes a look at other issues within the broader gay, lesbian, bisexual, transgender, and questioning community, including those unique to transgendered people, elders and youth—all as it relates to the marriage discussion. Some of the issues deal with gender identification and the challenges that may or may not arise as couples contemplate marriage.

Chapter 10 offers counsel and guidelines for finding qualified LGBT-savvy advisors to aid you in sorting out the issues identified here that may arise, whether or not you decide to wed.

Chapter 11 suggests some future litigation that will likely arise as a result of the complexities described in the earlier chapters and looks ahead to the future of the marriage equality movement.

## *Whether to Wed: Consider Love*

On the question of whether to wed, I believe it is important to point out that there are, of course, many reasons beyond taxes and financial or estate planning to consider when contemplating marriage. Love and commitment, for instance, are among these and, indeed, are perhaps more important. I do not pretend to supplant love by the analysis of whether to wed in this book, but merely park it at the door to concentrate on the concrete and practical aspects of considering whether to wed from a legal, tax, and financial planning perspective. The love and commitment piece is up to you . . . *

## *Why Marriage?*

Gay activists from around the country continually debate whether marriage equality is even the best strategy for legal recognition of same-sex couples. It is fraught with all the issues we know about, namely confusion with religious and historical views of marriage. Indeed, there was a push early on to "settle" for civil unions or domestic partnerships instead, so long as all the same legal rights and privileges were present. I will not elaborate further on this debate (which continues) other than to acknowledge it exists.

Personally, I subscribe wholeheartedly to the view that marriage matters. My friend, Jonathan Rauch, in his important work, *Gay Marriage: Why It Is Good for Gays, Good for Straights and Good for America,* articulates more clearly (and eloquently) than I could why marriage matters. Among other things, he makes the point that it is a "win-win-win." He says, "It is good for homosexuals, good for heterosexuals and good for the institution of marriage: good, in other words, for American society." It does this, he explains, by "shoring up the key values and commitments on which couples and families and societies depend." I trust that what you find in this book will help reinforce this notion.

---

* For a more detailed discussion on a recent survey of why gay couples choose to get married see http://www.pewsocialtrends.org/2013/06/13/a-survey-of-lgbt-americans/5/#chapter-4-marriage-and-parenting. This research shows that 84 percent of gay adults and 88 percent of all adults view love as a very important reason to get married. Interestingly, 46 percent of gay respondents, however, found the legal rights and benefits also an important reason for marriage—as opposed to 23 percent of their straight counterparts.

My favorite and most succinct articulation of a response to this question about why marriage matters came early on in our national debate from author and commentator Andrew Sullivan, in his fine essay published by *Time* magazine (February 8, 2004): "Why the M Word Matters." He said something that so profoundly resonated with me and touched my soul that our best man had the wisdom to read it as part of the toast at our wedding.

I share it here:

> *"As a child, I had no idea what homosexuality was. I grew up in a traditional home—Catholic, conservative, middle class. Life was relatively simple: education, work, family. I was raised to aim high in life, even though my parents hadn't gone to college. But one thing was instilled in me. What mattered was not how far you went in life, how much money you earned, how big a name you made for yourself. What really mattered was family and the love you had for one another. The most important day of your life was not graduation from college or your first day at work or a raise or even your first house. The most important day of your life was when you got married. It was on that day that all your friends and all your family got together to celebrate the most important thing in life: your happiness—your ability to make a new home, to form a new but connected family, to find love that put everything else into perspective."*

For those of you reading this book for whom marriage is a real possibility, if this book helps you get to that most important day, then I am pleased to have helped in some small way.

## A Friendly Disclaimer

It is important to note, that while I discuss the meaning, content, and use of legal and tax issues, documents, directives and such, nothing in this book should be considered legal/tax advice upon which you should rely in making important decisions about your life. I encourage you to consult your personal attorney and/or tax advisor before proceeding with any decisions that affect you and your loved ones. In Chapter 10, I offer some suggestions for how to find qualified professionals who understand and can help you plan for the unique issues that arise with same-sex couples.

Finally, to ensure compliance with requirements imposed by the U.S. Internal Revenue Service, I inform you that any tax advice contained in this book (including any updates) was not intended or written to be used, and cannot be used, by any taxpayer for the purpose of (1) avoiding tax-related penalties under the U.S. Internal Revenue Code or (2) promoting, marketing or recommending to another party any tax-related matters addressed herein. Again, I encourage the reader to consult with his/her own personal legal and tax professional advisor(s) before making important decisions based on material presented herein.

# CHAPTER 1

# About Marriage

*"When people talk about gay marriage, they miss the point. This isn't about gay marriage. It's about marriage. It's about family. It's about love. It isn't about religion. It's about civil marriage licenses. Churches can and should have the right to say no to marriage for gays in their congregations, just as Catholics say no to divorce, but divorce is still a civil option. These family values are not options for a happy and stable life. They are necessities. Putting gay relationships in some other category—civil unions, domestic partnerships, whatever—may alleviate real human needs, but by their very euphemism, by their very separateness, they actually build a wall between gay people and their families. They put back the barrier many of us have spent a lifetime trying to erase."*

—Andrew Sullivan in an essay in *Time* magazine,
"Why the M Word Matters to Me"

Marriage means different things to different people and its meaning in society has evolved over the centuries. To some, it means the very public declaration of having taken a life partner, a "mate" for life. To others, it is the true start of adulthood—of starting a new family separate from one's parents. Marriage can be about the benefits couples enjoy from having officially "tied the knot," such as Social Security and tax benefits, or inheritance rights. Or it can be about support from their family, friends, and community that couples typically enjoy when they wed. However, for most couples who decide to marry, the act itself typically goes beyond tangible rights, benefits, and public recognition; it creates an intangible bond that enriches and strengthens a loving relationship.

Yet, while establishing life-long, loving relationships is possible for nearly all humans, for centuries, marriage and all its associated rights and benefits were only available to heterosexual couples. The reasons for such restrictions date back to ancient times.

## The Origins of Marriage[1]

St. Augustine, sometime around 419 AD[2] appears to have come up with three commonly suggested justifications for marriage that seem to have stuck (in order of priority): *Proles* (procreation); *Fides* (fidelity or avoiding fornication); and *Sacramentum* (a permanent bond). This then led to the discussion of whether sex was only for the purpose of procreation within marriage (as the monks in medieval times thought), or whether sex could be for pleasure (if done within the confines of marriage). There were some who thought, however, that the pleasure should only be for the male—thus the concept of the "marital debt," which must be paid by the wife.

It wasn't until the early Protestant Reformation that the concept of marriage—not as a sacred or mystical institution, but as a secular cer-emony—was introduced. Indeed, one of the first definitions of marriage (which has now become known as modern or contemporary marriage) was offered by England's Archbishop Cranmer in 1549: "[The purpose of marriage is] mutual society, help and comfort, that one ought to have of the other, both in prosperity and in adversity."

## The Role of Procreation

In agrarian societies, marriage was more about allocation of work than love. Aristocratic families arranged marriages to combine certain properties or to protect them. For the less well-off, marriage was about providing help on the farm, or in the home or family business. Inseparable from each of these justifications for marriage, and intertwined with marriage generally, is the concept of procreation. Joining together man and woman was about creating the next generation.

Debates among religions abound about the relationship of sex and marriage and, in particular, the question of sex for procreation versus pleasure. Jewish rabbis, for instance, believed God had created human beings as flesh, intending both sexual pleasure and the ability to procreate by right, *B'rashit*, from the beginning. One Jewish marriage guide from the thirteenth century suggested that contraception was good if at least a few children were produced from a marriage.

It has been, however, the debate about contraception that spun marriage on its head during modern times. In the early nineteenth century, after Charles Goodyear invented the rubber condom (and made a fortune!), the debate really raged. It concluded with a number of states passing laws outlawing contraception on the theory that it would be criminal to have sex for anything other than procreative purposes. To do otherwise, even within the confines of marriage, would be to permit sex for love and pleasure, instead of for the procreative duty.

While that issue was finally settled by the Supreme Court's holding in *Griswold v. Connecticut*, which struck down laws outlawing contraception, the debate about marriage being for procreation continues today. Our current sitting Supreme Court debated it at some length during oral argument* in the recent *Perry* case, which presented the question of whether there is a constitutional right of same-sex couples to be married:

---

* As a member of the Supreme Court Bar, I had the honor to be present for oral arguments inside the Court for both the *Perry* and *Windsor* cases. My initial reflections, the day after, can be found on the *Huffington Post's* Blog: http://www. huffingtonpost.com/scott-e-squillace/scotus-gay-marriage_b_2967739.html.

> *JUSTICE KAGAN: Mr. Cooper, could I just understand your argument. In reading the briefs, it seems as though your principal argument is that same-sex and . . . opposite-sex couples are not similarly situated because opposite-sex couples can procreate, same-sex couples cannot, and the State's principal interest in marriage is in regulating procreation. Is that basically correct?*

> *MR. COOPER: . . . Your Honor, that's the essential thrust of our . . . position, yes.*

There is no doubt that an element of marriage has always been about procreation. It is clear, however, that unless we plan to fertility-test straight couples and only issue marriage licenses to the fertile couples who intend to procreate, civil marriage is not just about that. (What is fascinating about this debate is the lack of acknowledgment of same-sex couples' desire to beget and raise children, with the protections of marriage, through use of alternative reproductive therapies). Interestingly, it was the *Griswold* Court that suggested that marriage is "intimate to the degree of being sacred," even if it did not create babies.

Society continues to struggle with not only the definition, but the purpose of marriage at its core. If it is a lifetime and sacred commitment, then how is divorce possible? If it is solely for procreation, then what about contraception or infertile couples? But if you define it as we do in modern times, with vows that promise: "To love, honor, and cherish; in sickness and in health; for better or for worse," then whether the vows are made between two men, two women, or two people of opposite genders matters little. Marriage today is about the joining of two people who love each other and who desire to build a life together. In other words, as my mother who has been married for over fifty-five years now refers to her children's spouses—marriage is about choosing your "mate" for life.

## The Difference between Civil and Religious Marriage

From a legal perspective, marriage was, for a very long time, about the wife's legal interest merging into that of the husband's so that they became one legal entity (known as the doctrine of coverture). However, the definition of marriage continues to change, and with it the rights and benefits that accompany it.

While people use the word "marriage" in both religious and civil contexts, it means very different things from a religious standpoint than it does from a civil law standpoint. As I discuss marriage in this book, I am generally referring to civil or legal marriage. Not the ritual; not the sacrament. While religious and civil marriage often overlap, they are not the same. Indeed, in many continental European countries, the distinction is much clearer. Couples often go to the city hall to be legally or "civilly" married by a governmental official for all the legal rights and privileges that attach, then go to their place of worship to celebrate a spiritual union in the presence of friends and family.

It is confusing to many, as we debate gay marriage, as to which type of marriage is being discussed—that is to say, whether there is some movement afoot to force institutional religions to recognize same-sex marriages. While there is no such initiative, the equal marriage movement has affected religious institutions. The Episcopal Church in the U.S., for example, has progressed from not allowing these marriages to be consecrated or blessed in their churches to now allowing them. Regardless, whatever any organized religion's view of same-sex marriage is or may become, it is quite separate from the legal or civil marriage rights that are discussed herein.

The law has made great progress during the societal evolution of these concepts, by first protecting the right to marry as a fundamental right guaranteed under the Constitution[3] to protecting the right to consensual sex between two adults as a right of privacy.[4] For same-sex couples, the broadening of the definition of marriage from a union between heterosexual couples to one that includes all couples, opens the door not only to equality in rights and benefits, but, more importantly for some, to recognition and acceptance.

# CHAPTER 2

# The Gay and Lesbian Community

For the purposes of this book, I consider gay people to be those who are physically and emotionally attracted to being with another person of the same gender, and who may have sex or other forms of intimate relationship with such person(s). Often, as the human instinct to mate kicks in, gay people, like straight people, couple up and form lasting and profound bonds in a couple relationship. One indicator of this is living together, though of course cohabitation is not required to be in a committed relationship (straight or gay) with someone else.

It is hard to gauge exactly how many individuals are personally affected by the equal marriage movement and recent Supreme Court decisions, because data on our community are scarce. Unlike other minority populations, where ethnicity or gender is often apparent, sexual orientation requires self-reporting. Indeed, many gay and lesbian people don't realize that they are gay or lesbian, or don't identify as such, for a large portion of their lives. This speaks more to how we are socialized than whether the attraction to one's own gender exists. Some people never "come out," or take decades to do so, while still others never identify themselves as gay or lesbian at all.

For those who do identify themselves as gay or lesbian, there are data. The United States Census Bureau measured "unmarried couples" living together for the first time in its 1990 Census. That year, the Census Bureau reported 145,130 same-sex couples living together in the U.S. In 2000, the Census reported 601,209 same-sex couples living together. In 2010, the Census reported more detailed findings: 646,000 same-sex couples living together, of which 115,064 reported also living with children.

Research conducted in 2011 at The Williams Institute at UCLA, a credible academic institution that conducts research and reports on a variety of LGBTQ-related issues, estimated that 3.5 percent of the total U.S. population, or just over 11 million people, self-identify as LGBT. Some researchers believe that the number of people who self-identify as LGBT n the U.S. today is much larger. There are not necessarily more gays since the Census Bureau started reporting data, only that more people are perhaps more open and willing to share their status with the government.

And yet, published studies and census data likely grossly under-report—and, therefore, underestimate—the number of same-sex couples residing in the United States today. It goes without saying that the number of self-identified gay people correlates not to how many of us there are, but rather to how many of us understand who we are and are prepared to share that fact. Indeed, part of the gay marriage story is the story of our community's process of coming out.

Since at least the late nineteenth century, people who identified as having or desiring sex with someone of the same gender have been viewed as a particular type of person in society—with a variety of names associated, not all of which were flattering. Over the course of the next century, the medical profession struggled with the classification, including considering homosexuality a psychiatric disorder with an array of views for a "cure."[1]

The AIDS epidemic of the 1980s and '90s thrust many gay men out of the closet—not always willingly—and the gay marriage debate has since enticed, or maybe permitted, more people to come out.

# History of the Gay Rights Movement
## as it Pertains to Marriage

For many years, same-sex relationships, or, more precisely, sexual acts between same-sex partners, were criminal.[2] Indeed, until December 1973, homosexual conduct was considered a psychiatric illness.[3] However, a quick study of human history reveals that homosexual behavior has been around for centuries, often implicitly or explicitly accepted by governments or society of the time. This was the case in ancient Roman and Greek cultures.[4] In ancient Greece, for example, relationships, often sexual, between older male mentors and younger boys was so common that it had a name—pederasty. In ancient Rome, same-sex relationships between men were part of everyday life; words did not exist to differentiate between homosexuality and heterosexuality. In fact, it has been reported that all emperors except Claudius took male lovers; that he did not was viewed as odd. Additionally, sexual orientation was not as much gender-specific as it was defined by the sexual role each individual assumed—active or passive. It is only in more recent history that same-sex love has been deemed deviant or unnatural.

The modern gay rights movement in the U.S. is commonly acknowledged to have begun with the Stonewall Riots in 1969.[5] On June 27, 1969, members of the New York City Police Department raided a gay bar, the Stonewall Inn, on Christopher Street in Greenwich Village. The gay and transgendered patrons resisted the police and a riot ensued for days in the surrounding area. That event began a series of events around the country that introduced the nation to the concept of "gay pride"[6]—mostly in gay epicenters, such as San Francisco and New York. This became what is now commonly known as the gay liberation movement. It is perhaps understandable why this coincided with other notable social movements of that era, including the women's liberation movement and the anti-war efforts surrounding the Vietnam War.

Gay-friendly urban centers were not the only venues where change began to percolate. In the years that followed the Stonewall Riots, gay and lesbian advocates sought, sometimes successfully, to challenge laws that were discriminatory in the areas of housing, employment, and public accommodations, just to name a few. However, marriage was not even contemplated as a right that could be won at the time. Gay and lesbian

9

couples had to resort to other measures to provide each other with some of the legal rights and responsibilities that straight couples found in marriage.

## Prior Efforts to Formalize Same-Sex Relationships

Until very recently, the only legal way gay and lesbian couples could attempt to protect each other with some form of legal recognition was through adoption, civil unions and domestic partnerships (where permitted), and through private contractual arrangements, such as joint ownership agreements outlining the parties' respective rights and obligations to one another. In addition, during the 1970s, '80s and '90s, it became common knowledge that gay couples should do wills or trusts, powers of attorney, and other healthcare documents in each other's favor to attempt to protect each other in the event of a serious illness, disability, or death. However, even these agreements were not legally enforceable in certain states, depending on what the actual and stated "consideration" for the agreement was. Many states make sexual conduct, particularly illegal sexual conduct, an invalid form of consideration and, therefore, the contract could be unenforceable by law.

### Adoption

While today considered unorthodox, one partner's adoption of the other has historically been one of the few ways same-sex couples could establish a legal relationship that permits automatic inheritance rights,[7] certain rights as a health-care agent, and (in some states) a reduction in inheritance tax.

For example, one Pennsylvania couple—John and Gregory—had been together for forty-five years, but lived in a state that did not permit same-sex marriages. So, to ensure they could establish a means of protecting each other financially, John, then age sixty-five, adopted Gregory, who was then age seventy-three. Officially, Gregory is now his son and, therefore, entitled to all the benefits an immediate relative would be.[8] There can be a number of problems with this solution, however, including inadvertently tripping up a state's criminal incest laws. For another thing, you cannot "divorce" your child—so—if the relationship sours, you're stuck with one another. Moreover, not every state allows this. For example, in 1984, New York's highest court prohibited a fifty-seven-year-old gay man from adopting his fifty-year-old male partner on the theory that the adoption was "patently incongruous to the application of the adoption laws," and the sexual nature of the relationship was "repugnant" to any parent-child relationship.[9]

## Domestic Partnerships

The concept of domestic partnerships was first created in the 1990s by private industry as a response by employers who wanted to provide some benefits, usually health insurance, to employees in committed, long-term relationships where no legal recognition status existed. Some forward-thinking human resource managers crafted criteria to reflect indicators of committed long-term relationships, such as owning property and/or living together; reciprocal decision making for health and financial matters in case of disability and other serious events. Meeting the criteria became something that triggered certain corporate benefits in lieu of having lawful recognition for the couple's status.* It was only later that some state legislatures attempted to provide quasi-marriage legal rights by enacting domestic partner legislation. Interestingly, while attempting to shadow marriage rights, benefits and obligations, this quasi-marriage status now falls short since most federal marriage rights do not extend to registered domestic partners.

Termed "the lowest level of relationship recognition" by EqualityMaine (one of the state-based advocacy groups for equal marriage rights), domestic partnerships are sometimes considered largely symbolic now and provide little in the way of benefits or rights in some states, while others afford domestic partners many of the same rights as those of opposite-sex married couples. Part of the problem is precisely

---

* One such forward acting company was my former employer, Levi Strauss & Co., headquartered in San Francisco, California. A proud leader in this area. In 1992, it was the only one of the Fortune 500 Companies that offered domestic partner benefits.

this inconsistent application of rights for what seems like the same term—depending on different state laws (or even corporate rules).

California was the first state to officially recognize domestic partnerships in 1999, followed by the District of Columbia in 2002, and several other states after that. The benefits of forming a domestic partnership vary greatly by state. Some states do not recognize them at all, and those that do may recognize them to varying degrees; if the couple leaves their home state, other states may not recognize the domestic partnership. Today, many employers offer domestic partner healthcare benefits, which was one of the main reasons couples established these partnerships early on. However, because the protection they provide can be limited and are not portable, domestic partners still need to take additional steps to protect themselves and their partner financially, legally, and medically.[10]

## Civil Unions

Prior to the watershed decision in Massachusetts legalizing same-sex marriage, there was considerable work done in Vermont to establish the same legal rights for same-sex couples that opposite-sex couples enjoy. In 2000, Vermont was the first state in the country to adopt civil union legislation granting, for state law purposes, all of the same rights, benefits and obligations as married couples after being required by its highest court to fashion a remedy to the unequal treatment of same-sex couples.[11] Since then, several other states have legalized civil unions as a way to afford same-sex couples all of the same rights, benefits and obligations of marriage as their straight counterparts (like New Jersey, for instance). While civil unions generally provide more protection and benefits than domestic partnerships, they are still a lesser alternative to marriage, which is recognized universally and carries with it some 1,138 federal benefits.[12] **Civil unions, like domestic partnerships do not afford same-sex couples any of these federal rights that attach only based on marriage**. The Supreme Court made that abundantly clear in the recent *Windsor* decision. Couples that form a civil union still need to take additional steps to make it clear what rights, responsibilities, and benefits their partner is entitled to, particularly if they are in a state that does not recognize that union, or if they have property in that state.

With more and more states now offering same-sex marriage, civil unions and domestic partnerships are being phased out in states that recognize them, and are being replaced by marriage. States, such as Delaware that recently legalized same-sex marriage will no longer perform civil unions. And in Maryland, couples in a registered civil union must either unregister, or automatically be converted to married status.

## Contracts

Contracts and legal documents prepared for same-sex couples were a way to give partners legal rights in the absence of marriage. Wills or trusts, where a beneficiary is designated; joint property agreements, where rights, responsibilities, and ownership were spelled out; powers of attorney; health care proxies; and other formal documents were tools gay and lesbian couples used to formalize their relationship in states where their relationship was not recognized. Although progress has been made in many states, there is still a need for this important work to be done—particularly if one lives in or owns property in a non-recognition state.

Of course, just because partners signed contracts did not mean others agreed to abide by them. Horror stories abound about doctors and hospitals, or surviving family members, undertakers, or other people in positions of authority who refused to acknowledge or recognize such documents that were put in place by the deceased.[13]

For example, in 2009 when Janice Langbehn's partner of eighteen years, Lisa Pond, was restrained and dying alone in a hospital bed in Florida, the hospital personnel refused to honor the legal documents that were prepared and presented to them without a court order.[14] The social worker explained that they were in an "anti-gay" city and state. Janice and the three adopted children they were raising together were initially refused access to their loved one.[15] In the lawsuit that later ensued, seeking compensatory damages, the court found no monetary damages were available, even though the hospital was wrong to not accept the legal documents to grant the same-sex partner access to the hospital room.

A similar thing happened in Maryland when Bill Flanigan was denied access to his dying (registered domestic) partner under California law, despite the valid healthcare power of attorney that he presented.[16]

Another sad example was that of Sherry Barone and Cynthia Friedman, who had been in a committed relationship for thirteen years when Cynthia died at age thirty-five, leaving Sherry, she thought, in charge of her burial arrangements. Cynthia's family intervened, and only after three years and a federal lawsuit was Sherry able to direct the inscription on Sherry's headstone to respect her wishes, identifying her as "beloved life partner," instead of "friend," which the parents preferred.[17]

These stories only further propelled the gay community to understand generally (and for the advocates within the community to understand precisely) why some legal recognition of these relationships was critical to being able to achieve the "pursuit of happiness" that is so much a part of our grand American promise.

## The March toward Public Acceptance of Same-Sex Marriage

Given the weaknesses of these alternatives to marriage, it is clear why many couples were waiting until their state offered the opportunity to be officially married. For some, the wait may be short; for others, it may not happen in this lifetime. However, now that the federal government recognizes valid same-sex marriages, it is likely we will see more movement (or "destination weddings") in recognition states for couples travelling in from their home non-recognition states to become married in order to get at least those new federal rights that have become available.

When we look at how public perception of same-sex relationships and marriage has changed—and how *quickly* it has changed—there is reason to hope for continued change among these non-recognition states. Not only are couples asking for—even demanding—the right to marry their life partner, but straight members of the community are standing with them. In many parts of the country, there is less of an "us-versus-them" mentality.

In the U.S., 2008 was also a turning point. According to a Gallup poll, that was the year that the majority of Americans found gay and lesbian relationships "morally acceptable." That figure rose from only 38 percent in 2002 to 54 percent in 2012.[18] As the report states, gay and lesbian relationships are "the new normal." According to one recent survey, it is estimated that 56 percent of gay men and 58 percent of lesbian women would like to get married if they could, and 27 percent of the combined gay and lesbian population say they are unsure.[19] A total of 60 percent of the gay and lesbian respondents to that same survey reported already being married, or wanting to become married, as compared to 76 percent of their straight counterparts, probably attributable to the fact that many gay and lesbian couples never thought marriage would be possible in their lifetime—or perhaps they are still concerned about whether it will be made available in their state.[20] Today's young gay community is more "out and proud" than ever before. Indeed, studies show that popular support for gay marriage is directly correlated to age. A *Washington Post*-ABC poll in March 2013 reported that 81 percent of Americans eighteen to twenty-nine believe gay marriage should be legal.[21] In the over–sixty-five age group, however, the number falls to a low of 44 percent. As today's youth begin to age, we can expect that acceptance should continue to rise overall.

Increased acceptance among the youth, however, only partly explains another dynamic we've seen—increasing acceptance among all age groups of gay marriage in the past decade. The May 2012 Gallup poll regarding same-sex marriage concluded that the majority of Americans support legalizing gay marriage. Even within generations, acceptance is rising. That is, despite low levels of support among older Americans, those levels are still higher than they were a decade ago. This means that, across all age groups, people are changing their minds about gay marriage.

A *Washington Post* report summarizes the current situation well: "Combine the fact that young people are heavily supportive of gay marriage and every generation is growing more in favor of legalization as they age, and you see why the numbers on gay marriage have moved so quickly—and why they aren't likely to ever reverse themselves."

# CHAPTER 3

# Legalizing Same-Sex Marriage

The concept of same-sex marriage is relatively new. The early days of the gay rights movement focused primarily on being identified and recognized as gay or lesbian so that discrimination in the areas of housing, employment, public accommodation, and other areas might cease. There was little effort at the time to formally recognize relationships. In fact, the general consensus through the 1990s was that gays and lesbians ought not push too hard for more than mere acknowledgment of the existence of their relationships. To ask for more might damage the progress the gay rights movement had made, leaders suggested at the time. Indeed, debate continues within the community about the place for civil union or domestic partner legislation in places that refuse to go further and allow full marriage rights to same-sex couples.

However, as early as 1971, the first gay couple sued for the legal right to marry, in Minnesota.[1] Richard Baker and James Michael McConnell were denied a marriage license by a county clerk, and challenged that denial on federal constitutional grounds—including equal protection and due process—citing marriage as a "fundamental right." The Minnesota Supreme Court refused to recognize this theory, citing, among other great and well-known legal authorities, *Webster's Third New*

*International Dictionary*'s definition of marriage, and the book of Genesis from the Bible. Baker and McConnell appealed to the Supreme Court, which denied their appeal "for want of a federal question"—in other words, denying that the two had a federal right to marry that the Court could protect. Since that time, advocates have attempted to seek recognition of same-sex relationships based on state constitutions, at least initially.

## Hawaii

It was not until the Hawaii Supreme Court took up the question in the early 1990s that any court issued a favorable ruling suggesting that gay couples indeed may have a constitutional right to marry.[2] The story behind this case demonstrates both the struggles couples have encountered, and the fortitude some have shown to pursue this right. It also demonstrates the legal wrangling that can go on and on for years as these important questions are considered in our constitutional democratic process. Summarized below is the Hawaii story, but many other states, like New York, California, and Maine, have similar ones.

In December of 1990, three couples filed their application for a marriage license in Hawaii. They otherwise met the statutory requirements for marriage in the state at the time, except for the fact that they were same-sex couples. Wanting cover, State Health Director John C. Lewin, whose agency administered issuance of marriage licenses, sought advice from the state's attorney general, who concluded that same-sex couples did not have a right to such license and therefore, the couples were denied. The couples filed suit in state court seeking an order for the licenses to be issued based on equal protection grounds. They argued, essentially, that the denial was gender-based discrimination, which was prohibited under the state's constitution. Ultimately, the justices of the Hawaii Supreme Court agreed. In May 1993, those justices remanded the case to the lower courts to have a trial to determine whether there was a compelling state interest at stake that could justify this discrimination, which they found was otherwise prohibited under the Hawaii Constitution.

Seeing where this might go, the state legislature quickly took up the question and passed a statute outlawing marriage licenses for same-sex couples and, interestingly, chartered a commission to study the question of what rights might be appropriate for same-sex couples. (That commission later recommended same-sex couples should be afforded the right to marry, and that comprehensive legislation should be enacted for same- and opposite-sex couples who chose not to be married, but who otherwise wanted to be together and protected under the law.)

This did not end the debate in Hawaii by a long shot. Years later, in 1996, a trial again was held in which the state of Hawaii put forth five state interests it claimed were sufficiently "compelling" to allow it to prohibit same-sex couples from marrying:

- Protecting the health and welfare of children and other persons;

- Fostering procreation within a marital setting;

- Securing or assuring recognition of Hawaii marriages in other jurisdictions;

- Protecting the state's public fiscal duties from the reasonably foreseeable effects of state approval of same-sex marriage in the laws of Hawaii;

- Protecting civil liberties, including the reasonably foreseeable effects of state approval of same-sex marriages on its citizens.

In the 1996 trial, each side presented expert witnesses with specialties in psychology, sociology, and childhood development. On December 3, 1996, Judge Kevin K.S. Chang ruled that the state had not established any compelling interest in denying same-sex couples the ability to marry and that, even if it had, it failed to prove that the Hawaii statute that had been adopted by the state legislators was narrowly tailored to avoid unnecessary abridgement of constitutional rights. He enjoined the state from refusing to issue marriage licenses to otherwise-qualified same-sex couples, but stayed (meaning "hit-the-pause button" on) his ruling, acknowledging the "legally untenable" position same-sex couples would be in if they married. The Hawaii Supreme Court reversed him on appeal.

Meanwhile, opponents of same-sex marriage in Hawaii had geared up for a ballot initiative to amend the state constitution to prohibit same-sex marriage, as a constitutional matter. The voters approved this on November 3, 1998, and the next year the Hawaii Supreme Court essentially let that be the final word—ordering Chang's ruling to be vacated.

A combination of Hawaii's Supreme Court ruling in 1993 and Judge Chang's lower court decision later in 1996 gave the United States Congress great concern that the legal arguments for same-sex marriage could indeed gain traction and therefore, in Congress' estimation, change the definition of marriage—including for federal purposes. This concern led, eventually, to the Defense of Marriage Act (DOMA).

## Enter Congress: The Federal Defense of Marriage Act (DOMA)

The Hawaii court cases gave rise to a national and rather public debate about whether homosexuals should have the legal right to marry.[3] Congress became actively involved in the debate in 1993, during President Bill Clinton's first term.

Not only did President Clinton have to maneuver carefully for his administration's overall legislative agenda, it was a presidential election year. So when Congress proposed and passed DOMA, Clinton signed it into law on September 21, 1996, presumably as a compromise for other items on his agenda.* Its purpose was to clarify the definition of marriage as being between a man and a woman, mollifying conservatives who valued the status quo. The *Congressional Record* reported that the purpose of the law was to:

> *"reflect an honor of collective moral judgment and to express moral disapproval of homosexuality."* [5]

---

\* President Clinton has since disavowed his endorsement of this legislation—some twenty years later when he said, "On March 27, DOMA will come before the Supreme Court, and the justices must decide whether it is consistent with the principles of a nation that honors freedom, equality and justice above all, and is therefore constitutional. As the President who signed the act into law, I have come to believe that DOMA is contrary to those principles and, in fact, incompatible with our Constitution."[4]

This would later haunt the adversaries of gay marriage when the case eventually came before the Supreme Court in March of 2013, where the law's defenders attempted to establish that DOMA was about more than just moral disapproval of, and discrimination against, gays and lesbians. Justice Elena Kagan read just this portion of the *Congressional Record* and asked whether this wasn't really what DOMA was all about.

DOMA essentially had two operative provisions:

- Section 2 permits states to refuse to honor same-sex marriages from another state. It says "[n]o State, territory, or possession of the United States, or Indian tribe, shall be required to give effect to any public act, record, or judicial proceeding of any other State, territory, possession, or tribe respecting a relationship between persons of the same-sex that is treated as a marriage under the laws of such other State, territory, possession, or tribe, or a right or claim arising from such relationship."

- Section 3 defines marriage for all federal purposes (benefits and otherwise) as between "one man and one woman," regardless of how any given state may choose to define marriage.[6] It says "[i]n determining the meaning of any Act of Congress, or of any ruling, regulation, or interpretation of the various administrative bureaus and agencies of the United States, the word 'marriage' means only a legal union between one man and one woman as husband and wife, and the word 'spouse' refers only to a person of the opposite sex who is a husband or a wife."

In effect, DOMA became the license to discriminate, at least with respect to all federal laws, against gay couples. What followed was a complex series of legislative actions in many states, more court cases and some ballot initiatives to change state constitutions—all of which is summarized in detail in Appendix A. It covers the history on a state-by-state basis. An important fact to note is that some thirty-six states adopted "mini-DOMA" statutes that mirrored the federal law for their state purposes before any court found same-sex couples had a right to be married.

## Then Came Vermont: Civil Unions

It was the Vermont Supreme Court, however, that took the bold step in December 1999 to find a constitutional right for same-sex couples to enjoy the same rights, privileges and obligations as their opposite sex counterparts, stopping short, however, of granting access to full marriage. In *Baker v. Vermont*[7], a case involving three same-sex couples seeking redress for having been denied marriage licenses, the Vermont Supreme Court found that its state constitution afforded these couples the same "benefits and protections" as opposite sex couples with respect to marriage and ordered the state legislature to create a solution consistent with its ruling. After an acrimonious debate, the Vermont legislature adopted the country's first Civil Union legislation that granted all of the same rights and benefits of marriage to same-sex couples who chose to register with the state under this new status. Governor Howard Dean signed the bill into law on April 26, 2000 at some considerable political expense to himself which would be realized later.[8]

The floodgates opened and couples from around the country flocked to Vermont to obtain this legal recognition status that was, in effect, largely symbolic outside of Vermont, but important for many nonetheless. In its first year some 2,479 couples registered their relationships with the state of which only 502 couples were resident of Vermont.[9] By October of 2004, just before the landmark case in Massachusetts granting full marriage rights, some 7,201 couples had registered.[10]

## Alas, Massachusetts: The First State to Legalize Same-Sex Marriage

The effect of DOMA, however, was not squarely felt until the now-famous landmark decision that came out of the Supreme Judicial Court of Massachusetts in November 2003 in which gay and lesbian couples were given the constitutional right to marry in the Commonwealth.

In her majority opinion in *Goodridge v. Dept. of Public Health*\*, Chief Justice Margaret Marshall wrote:[11]

> *"The Massachusetts Constitution affirms the dignity and equality of all individuals. It forbids the creation of second-class citizens . . . Barred access to the protections, benefits and obligations of civil marriage, a person who enters into an intimate, exclusive union with another of the same-sex is arbitrarily deprived of membership in one of our community's most rewarding and cherished institutions. The exclusion is incompatible with the constitutional principles of respect for individual autonomy and equality under law."*

Massachusetts, therefore, became the first state in the union to begin issuing marriage licenses to same-sex couples on May 17, 2004. (Interestingly, the effective date for the first lawful marriages in Massachusetts was exactly fifty years to the day of the anniversary of the Supreme Court's landmark ruling in *Brown v. Board of Education*,[12] in which the Court established the principle that "separate but unequal" is not acceptable in these United States.)

The reaction nationally was loud and profound. While the backlash had long since been underway since Hawaii, with federal DOMA legislation and thirty-six mini-DOMAs in states, as well as four states enshrining discrimination in their state constitutions even before *Goodridge* was decided,

---

\* This thoughtful decision was no accident. For years, smart and dedicated advocates carefully strategized about bringing this case. I would be remiss if I did not acknowledge the enormous contributions from my friends at GLAD in Boston—Gay and Lesbian Advocates and Defenders (www.glad.org). While many worked on this case, including attorneys Gary Buseck and Jennifer Levi, the genius behind it was my friend, Mary Bonauto, who actually argued the case before the Supreme Judicial Court and whom the *New York Times* compared to Justice Thurgood Marshall: "Bonauto's patient, quietly passionate yet self-effacing advocacy may have as far-reaching an effect on America as did that of Thurgood Marshall." http://www.nytimes.com/2004/05/09/magazine/toward-a-more-perfect-union. html?pagewanted=all&src=pm. Mary was also the architect and lawyer for the Vermont Civil Union case that some believed paved the way for all of the legal recognition cases to happen. Many other advocacy groups, including the ACLU, Lambda Legal, Freedom to Marry, and the state marriage equality organizations have also worked tremendously hard to secure equal marriage rights for us all.

the decision did galvanize conservatives around the country to react. From the moment the decision was made, then-Governor Romney and conservatives from around the country admonished the "activist judges" in Massachusetts for upsetting "thousands of years of history" of the institution of marriage. While recent modern history has shown some stability to the social understanding of marriage between one man and one woman for the purpose of love, commitment, and sometimes procreation, a brief study of the institution quickly shows that it has changed dramatically over the years from being about property and worker support (in agrarian societies) toward equality.

On June 22, 2004, Governor Romney testified before the U.S. Senate Judiciary Committee, urging its members to protect the definition of marriage by saying: "Marriage is not an evolving paradigm, but is a fundamental and universal social institution that bears a real and substantial relation to the public health, safety, morals, and general welfare of all of the people of Massachusetts." Governor Romney then proceeded to push for a constitutional amendment in Massachusetts that mirrored the federal DOMA, defining marriage in the Commonwealth as between "one man and one woman" only (this amendment was also referred to as a "mini-DOMA").

John Adams, one of the architects of the Massachusetts Constitution, intended any amendments to it to be thoughtfully done and to require a process that included input from elected representatives and from the people themselves. Therefore, in order to amend its constitution, the Massachusetts state legislature had to convene an extraordinary session of both houses in a constitutional convention to debate and vote (by a two-thirds majority) on the amendment—in two consecutive terms. Adams' process did what it was intended to do, and clear-headed, rational thought won out over the initial backlash against the Massachusetts court decision.

The first constitutional convention to consider the amendment occurred in 2004, where the amendment passed. However, between the first constitutional convention and the second in 2005, groups around the state worked to unseat legislators who voted for the amendment—and in the second constitutional convention, the amendment failed. There was a subsequent attempt to undo the effect of this important case by a citizen-initiated amendment that passed initially in 2006 and then failed in 2007. The final vote in June 2007 saw support of over three-fourths of the state legislature in support of marriage equality. The proposal to amend the Massachusetts Constitution to define marriage as only between one man and one woman, therefore, never reached the ballot for a popular vote, and further attempts to amend the constitution by ballot initiative have all failed in Massachusetts. The right of same-sex couples to marry in Massachusetts is solidly secure now as we celebrate a decade of same-sex marriages in the Commonwealth.

In the first year that same-sex marriages were legal in Massachusetts, 6,200 took place. The following year, in 2005, the number fell (presumably because the first year included decades of pent-up demand) to 1,900, of which 64 percent were lesbians. In 2006 and 2007, the total number of marriages in the state evened out at around 1,500 per year, representing about 4 percent of the average 36,000 marriages that occur in the state annually.[13] The divorce rate among same-sex couples is difficult to quantify, only because the option to marry is so new; recent statistics indicate same-sex divorce is still relatively rare.[14]

Other states have had different experiences in establishing and defeating mini-DOMAs; the state-by-state battle continues with efforts by state legislatures, popular ballot initiatives and court cases continuing every day around the country.

The national debate begun about same-sex marriage in the early 1990s continues today. Some have argued that the effect of this debate has had ramifications in the broader political context. For example, Harvard Professor Michael Klarman, author of *How Same-Sex Marriage Came to Be*, has suggested that the debate about same-sex marriage may have been the cause for many conservative Ohioan voters to come out in support of its "mini-DOMA" in 2004. This was at the same time that President George Bush was fighting for his second term, and the same-sex marriage issue was the most important reason he won those electoral votes.[15] This theory, however, has been strongly debated by other legal scholars. For example, Duke University Professor D. Sunshine Hillygus and University of Arkansas Professor Todd Shields reviewed 2004 post-election data and concluded that the gay marriage issue had little or no effect on voter decisions, but instead, the drivers were really the war in Iraq, the economy and terrorism.[16] In fact, some have argued that even if the *Goodridge* decision galvanized the *uber*-Republicans to react, it may have done more long-term damage to the party, since young people overwhelmingly favor legal recognition of same-sex marriage. As a result, they may find the Republican party less attractive. Indeed, President Obama's endorsement of gay marriage during his recent, and hotly contested, re-election bid seemed to have no discernible negative effect to his ability to be re-elected to a second term.

The battle, however, to dismantle DOMA at the federal level had to take place in our country's highest court. While a number of important cases were brought and worked their way up to the Supreme Court on this issue, including two from Massachusetts, which were among the first federal cases to successfully challenge the constitutionality of DOMA on a federal level, only one was taken up by the Court to be heard in March of 2013.

## The Story of Edith Windsor and Thea Spyer

Edith Windsor and Thea Spyer had been together forty-five years and engaged for forty when they were married in 2007 in Toronto, Canada. They had long been a couple committed to one another, having spent the majority of their lives together. They exchanged diamond brooches in 1967 when they became engaged (so as not to arouse suspicion or questions about an assumed future husband); they lived together near Washington Square in Manhattan; and bought property together in Southampton.[17] Their lives were already intertwined. They didn't need marriage to validate their relationship. "So why get married then?" they were repeatedly asked. "I was seventy-seven, Thea was seventy-five," Windsor says, "but the fact is that everybody treated it as different. It turns out marriage is different."

In an interview with *The Guardian*, on the very day the Supreme Court announced its decision in her case, Windsor went on to say, "I've asked a number of long-range couples, gay couples who . . . got married, I've asked them: 'Was it different the next morning?' and the answer is always: 'Yes. It's a huge difference.'"[18]

While Windsor and Spyer may have felt different about their relationship once they were officially married, their government did not.

According to the federal government, under DOMA, two women could not be recognized as married in the eyes of the federal government. Although it did not matter much to the women then what the government believed, it made a huge difference to them financially by 2009, the year Spyer passed away.

In fact, the impetus for Windsor and Spyer's wedding was Spyer's declining health. Having been diagnosed with multiple sclerosis in 1977, at age forty-five, Spyer had increasingly relied on her life partner for care and support. When doctors gave her just a year to live, Windsor and Spyer decided they wanted to finally formalize their union. Less than two years later, Spyer died, bequeathing her entire estate to her lawfully-wedded wife. Fortunately, by 2009, New York State had begun to recognize "foreign same-sex marriages," meaning marriages lawfully entered into outside of New York, so Windsor and Spyer's marriage was recognized by the state they lived in.

Unfortunately, because their marriage was not recognized by the federal government, however, Spyer's estate was hit with an estate tax of $363,053 due and payable to the U.S. Treasury by her surviving spouse, as executrix of the estate, within nine months of the date of Spyer's death. Windsor quickly learned that it was more than any opposite-sex spouse would have been required to pay; no lawfully married opposite-sex couple would have been required to pay the tax under similar circumstances.[19] Legally, she was treated as a friend who had been given a gift, rather than a wife and mate entitled to the inheritance tax-free. Still grieving, but growing angrier at the treatment she was receiving, Windsor decided to fight the tax bill.

In June 2013, the highest court in the land ruled in her favor. The United States Supreme Court declared that the Defense of Marriage Act violated the U.S. Constitution's equal protection clause. She and Spyer *had* been married and she was entitled to a refund of the overpayment of all of the estate taxes paid.

It was a major win, not only for Edith Windsor and the memory of her late spouse, but for all other same-sex couples already married or who are considering marriage. The truth is, there are hundreds of thousands, maybe even millions, of same-sex couples who may be impacted by this landmark decision.

## The Pace of Change Quickens

Instead of settling for civil unions and other second-class forms of marriage, same-sex couples began demanding the same rights as other couples—which has led to a combination of court cases, ballot initiatives, and legislation bringing the issue of same-sex marriage to the fore. This process has been driven by, and is driving, increasing acceptance of same-sex relationships among the American public. Rising numbers of Americans agree that offering gay and lesbian couples the opportunity to marry was only fair; universal support for same-sex marriage continues to climb.

Does this mean that all fifty states will soon recognize same-sex marriages and offer them to their residents? Sadly, no. But the pace of change is increasing, and that is a major step in the right direction. More states are likely to at least recognize marriages performed in other states, while others have a long way to go before marriage of its same-sex residents will be approved. It is possible that another case will come before the Supreme Court raising the question, like in *Perry*, about whether there is a constitutional right (federally) of all same-sex couples to be married. If that case is successful, the recalcitrant states won't have a choice but to acquiesce to a new reality.[20]

Interestingly, in the wake of the Supreme Court rulings of 2013, more people believe that same-sex marriage is more widely accepted than it actually is. On the East and West Coasts, the majority of Americans support same-sex marriage and assume such support is universal nationwide. Unfortunately, that is not the case. The majority of states still prohibit same-sex marriage.

One need only look at other instances of macro-social change to understand the pace at which such societal shifts occur. While women's suffrage may have appeared to happen overnight, the time period between the start of the women's suffrage movement to women being given the right to vote was seventy-two years, from 1848 to 1920; essentially, a generation. Such wide-scale change takes time. Likewise, it wasn't until 1967 that the

Supreme Court struck down prohibitions against interracial marriage. For centuries before, it was legal—and not uncommon—for states to forbid marriage between individuals of different races.

In both examples, support for such change percolated among the states, rising in popularity until a Supreme Court decision instituted change. Many Americans thought such changes were the end of the world. Their whole perspective on gender roles and ethnicity were turned upside down. Yet in a matter of years, the issue seemed to have faded into the distance. Whatever had stood in the way of women voting or interracial couples marrying is long gone. Often that barrier is generations of Americans with long-held beliefs and prejudices; as the next generation comes along, the consensus shifts. That is what we are witnessing now.

# CHAPTER 4

# Whether to Wed: Federal Legal and Tax—Pros and Cons

There are many reasons to consider getting married, not the least of which are the more than 1,000 federal rights and benefits now available to you and your spouse should you decide to take this step. While it is clear that all of these rights, obligations and benefits apply instantly to those who reside in a recognition state, the reverse is more confusing. Not all federal benefits extend to same-sex married couples who are living in a non-recognition state; most do, however, and the list is increasing. (In Chapter 6, I outline in more detail those federal rights that stem from "place of celebration" versus "place of domicile".)

The fact that a couple from a non-recognition state can now travel to a recognition state, get married and return home with many of these federal rights, even though their home state may not recognize their marriage, is perhaps the biggest news to come out of the landmark *Windsor* case from the Supreme Court recently. But, every couple needs to carefully consider the pros and cons of this decision and the consequences. What follows in this and the next two chapters is a detail analysis of these pros and cons from a federal and state law perspective.

Summarized here are some of the most important factors in terms of federal rights or benefits to weigh in your decision-making process about whether to wed.

## The Pros of Getting Married—Federal Benefits

The list of federal benefits and responsibilities now available to married same-sex couples is a long one, and it continues to change. The list we discuss here is current as of our late 2013 writing date. It will no doubt be updated in subsequent editions.* Some of these rights and benefits apply only to those married and living in "recognition" states—and others extend further. For the balance, we await guidance from the appropriate federal agency or further guidance from the courts.

For anyone considering whether to wed, it is important to keep track of your own list of federal benefits and consequences that apply to you. Some of these considerations apply to all couples, but many are specific and may or may not apply to your own personal situation. More importantly, not everyone gives each factor the same weighted importance as the next person in determining whether to get married. Those closer to retirement, for example, may greatly value the ability to receive the spousal survivor benefits for Social Security. At the end of the day, it is for you to decide, ideally, with the input of trusted advisors who understand your personal financial and tax situation.

The following are the issues married couples must face and the federal benefits they may receive by deciding to wed:

## Federal Taxes (Generally)

As the summer of 2013 drew to its close, the Thursday before Labor Day weekend, the IRS released an announcement that sent a sigh of relief across the country: It would recognize all same-sex marriages for all federal tax purposes—regardless of where the couple lives (or dies). While consistent with past practices (including recognition of common law marriages

---

* For more current updates, visit: www.whethertowed.com

when couples moved to states that didn't recognize them), this ruling was nonetheless monumental.[1] Tax practitioners everywhere are still sorting out what this means for same-sex couples already married, since for some it is good news, and others not (at least from an income tax perspective.) There may also be retroactive benefits or implications for same-sex couples who were already married. For sure, this was terrific news from a gift and estate tax perspective, as explained more fully below. It was also a great victory for advocates of marriage equality, and it will have broad ramifications.[2]

One of the ramifications of this announcement is that prior taxes paid that shouldn't have been can now be refunded (if you apply soon!). For example, for years, corporate employers offered same-sex partner benefits for health insurance. Those benefits were "imputed" into the income of the employed spouse—and the value of that benefit was subject to additional federal income tax. If you are still within the applicable statute of limitations (generally three years, but you need to consult your accountant), you will now be eligible for a refund for the taxes paid on those benefits. You may, however, become subject to what is commonly referred to as "the marriage penalty" by filing jointly.

## Income Tax

Taxes, taxes, and more damn taxes. They are the source of much consternation for many reasons. Before I elaborate on the income tax issues gay couples may face if they choose to marry, it may be helpful to remember that there are two fundamentally different tax systems in the U.S. today that operate in tandem: 1) The income tax system—which requires us all to report our annual income and any associated payments due by April 15 of each year; and 2) The transfer tax system—which is seldom on the radar screen until it is too late. The transfer tax system includes (possible) gift taxes during one's lifetime and estate and generation-skipping taxes at death.

This discussion regarding income tax is not meant to substitute good advice from qualified tax professionals. You will hear again and again that everyone's situation is different—and it is! You may have different income levels, deductions, different cost basis in your assets, etc., so please, before deciding anything based on the effect marriage would have on your taxes, please consult a qualified tax professional.

Here are the high-level issues to consider:

First, it is important to consider whether marriage will create higher or lower income tax costs for you as a couple. When one is filing as single there is an effective tax rate on which your income is taxed. Often it's a number like 15 percent or 24 percent or 33 percent of your total income. However, when a couple is married, they must file as married (and can only elect to file jointly or separately—but always married). All income (and available deductions) is combined into one bucket and the rate is then determined based on the combined income and deductions. So, in the very traditional marriages of the 1950s, when it was common for one spouse to work at home (typically raising the children) and one outside of the home, as a salaried employee, the combination of the two "incomes" could allow the couple to achieve a lower marginal tax rate. That is, the taxes a single person would pay would be higher than a married couple earning the same level of income, since the average of the two incomes (with only one generating an income from outside the home) was lower on a per person basis.

However, when both spouses in a couple are earning wages, particularly higher wages, then the combination of the two may bring them to a combined higher marginal rate, and may cause their itemized deductions to be phased out sooner. It also could cause the couple to trigger the alternative minimum tax (AMT), which generally will increase a taxpayer's tax bill. All of these consequences are commonly referred to as the "marriage penalty" in the income tax world. The net effect is that a married couple may indeed be subject to higher income tax liability if married than they would have been if they were single. Now that the federal government rocognizes same-sex marriages, there is no "single option," only whether to file jointly or separately—but always as married, as mentioned. It is generally more costly for a married couple to file separately than to file jointly, with some exceptions. There are terrific (easy-to-use) consumer software applications available to help run the numbers to show which is better for your situation, like Turbo Tax®.

# Two Examples about Marriage's Effect on Income taxes—Sarah and Beth, and Brad and Matt

In light of the recent change in IRS rules for same-sex married couples, all such couples, irrespective of where they reside, now have the option to file their income tax returns either as married filing jointly, or married filing separately, rather than as single taxpayers. Almost always, married filing jointly (MFJ) is better than married filing separate (MFS) and is explained more fully below.

However, what many couples struggle with is the threshold question of whether they will be in a better or worse position, from an income tax perspective, if they choose to get married, since they could get hit with the "marriage penalty" by being married. This depends largely on whether both are working outside the home and earning similar salaries, or whether one spouse is earning significantly more, either because the other has a lower-paying job, or is at home caring for children.

Provided below are two examples of the federal income tax effect of marriage. First, we illustrate how Sarah and Beth are better off (income tax wise) as a result of marriage (the "marriage bonus"). We then show an example of the federal income tax effect for Brad and Matt, who are worse off (income tax wise) as a result of marriage (the "marriage penalty").

Sarah and Beth are contemplating getting married. Sarah is the CEO of a privately held company, and Beth works part-time as a teacher's aide, but is the primary caregiver for their two children, who are still in school. Below are their current salaries and the calculations of what their federal income tax exposure would be if they stay single or get married. (Note, for purposes of this example, we kept it simple and did not include the effect of state income taxes on these projections, which could have an effect. We used 2013 tax rates for this illustration.)

Sarah salary and bonus: $250,000

Beth salary: $12,500

Sarah's federal taxes if single: $61,750

Beth's federal taxes if single: $250

The total combined federal tax bill for them then when single therefore is $62,000 but if they get married, their total combined federal taxes (filing jointly) would be $55,001 for a total savings of $6,999—or a "marriage bonus."

The reason this occurs is that Sarah is at the 33 percent marginal tax rate as a single filer, but when they get married, a greater portion of her income gets taxed at the lower rates. By combining their incomes as a married couple, their tax liability is effectively averaged across both spouses, resulting in a lower total bill, since some of Sarah's higher income can be taxed at a lower marginal effective rate.

The marriage penalty occurs when both spouses earn relatively the same, or when the combination pushes them into a higher tax bracket.

Let's look at another example:

Example 2: Brad and Matt are also contemplating marriage. Brad is a partner in a law firm, and Matt works in the financial services industry. They do not have children yet. (We used the same assumptions as in Example 1 above.)

Brad's salary: $185,000

Matt's salary: $210,000

Brad's federal taxes, if single: $42,293

Matt's federal taxes, if single: $50,221

Combined as single taxpayers, they pay a total of $92,514 in federal income taxes. If they get married, however, their combined federal tax liability would become $103,324, which is an increase in total federal tax liability of $10,810. This is an example of the "marriage penalty."

As single guys, they were at lower effective marginal rates. Brad was at an effective rate of 24 percent and Matt at 25 percent, but when they combine their incomes and file jointly, their total effective rate becomes 26.4 percent. The reason for this is that combining their incomes pushes them both into higher marginal rates. Certain itemized deductions also become phased out at the higher rates that would have been allowed as single taxpayers. This causes their tax bill to go up as a result of their marriage.

While a marriage bonus can occur when there is a major discrepancy between what each spouse earns, the so-called marriage penalty occurs when both spouses earn relatively the same and the combination pushes them into a higher tax bracket. Instead of reducing the total tax liability when both incomes are combined, the marginal tax rate often goes up when the household income comes close to doubling. In general, the result is a higher tax rate and a higher total tax bill.

## Whether to File (when Married) Separate or Jointly?

If you are married, irrespective of where you live, the IRS will now require you to file married and the only choice is whether to file married jointly or married separately. Some of the most common reasons that married couples choose to file separate tax returns include medical expenses, risk, and the potential for divorce. If one of you has high, un-reimbursed medical expenses, it is possible that filing separately would make it possible to deduct them. These deductions need to exceed 7.5 percent in 2012, or 10 percent in 2013, of your adjusted gross income, which is easier to hit when applied to only one salary; filing jointly might makes it more difficult to exceed the 7.5 percent minimum.* Or if your spouse is more agressive with deductions than you are, it may be smart to separate yourself from the potential liability to protect yourself from any tax liability later. And if your relationship is tenuous, it may be smarter to begin separating any tax liabilities now.

However, by filing separately, some of the deductions and credits you forfeit include the following:[3]

- Child and dependent care credit
- College tuition deduction
- American Opportunity Tax Credit
- Student loan interest deduction
- Earned income tax credit

---

* Also the 7.5 percent applies to the regular tax calculation in 2012, but AMT is at 10 percent and will then match the regular tax calculation beginning in 2013, but for the exception noted.

- Tax-free exclusion of U.S. bond interest
- Tax-free exclusion of Social Security benefits
- Credit for the elderly and disabled

It's always smart to run the numbers both ways, to see which filing status makes the most sense each year. And, for anyone with any level of complexity, I strongly advise you to seek advice from a qualified professional tax preparer (CPA) who actually specializes is these issues for same-sex couples.

There may be some mitigating factors for a couple that could inform a better income tax position if filing jointly. For example, assuming one spouse has accumulated capital losses (that are being carried forward), they are limited to claiming a loss in excess of their gains of only $1,500 per year. Assuming their spouse has realized a great deal of capital gains, then filing jointly would allow their gains and losses to be combined and help to reduce the couple's capital gain tax overall.

There are a few other benefits to married couples from an income tax perspective. For example, any gain realized upon the sale of a principal residence is not taxed up to the first $250,000 of gain. That amount is doubled for a married couple filing jointly—regardless of whose name the house may be titled in or purchased by. This is sometimes important when couples have had real estate for many years and hold highly appreciated property.*

If you do decide to get married, remember to revisit your withholdings election with your employer to reflect your new tax filing status—married, either filing jointly or separately. Consult with your CPA about which option would be better for your personal situation. Marital status for tax filings is always determined based on your marital status on the last day of the tax year. So, if you are married by December 31, you can, in your filings the following April 15, claim married status for the entire prior year!

---

* See IRC Section 121 for more information about exclusion of gain from sale of principal residence and for information relating to the "ownership" and "use" requirements.

Remember that going forward, any partner/spouse health benefits that are provided by your employer will no longer be considered "imputed income" to you and subject to additional taxation.

A word about divorce and taxes. Prior to the *Windsor* case, same-sex couples who needed to get divorced got the double whammy. Not only did they have to go through the process their state required for a divorce, which is sometimes long and painful. They might also have been made to make payments in the form of a divorce settlement or alimony that was subject to gift taxes, and not excluded from income taxes by the payer, since the federal government treated the couple as legal strangers. I cover the gift tax issues below, but gift taxes were sometimes tripped by a divorce as a result of this treatment. If a couple had been subject to this, it is worth considering amending prior tax returns to un-do that treatment.

Post-DOMA, divorce payments (including alimony) are now deductible by the payor. Also, previously, retirement plan benefits were not easily split or allocated in a divorce because of the federal rules in this area. Now they can be split without adverse tax consequences.

## Transfer Taxes: Gift, Estate and Generation-Skipping Tax

Sometimes referred to as the "death tax," the estate tax kicks in only after someone has died and leaves an estate to others. There was considerable discussion about this in recent political elections, and some may recall that part of the grand compromise in 2012 to extend the Bush-era tax credits included extending the estate tax credits. What this means, in effect, is that the federal estate tax is now only something applicable to the very wealthy in our country. It applies to estates that exceed $5.25 million (per person) or $10.5 million for married couples.* I always like to tell clients this is a nice problem to have. (The estate tax rate, however, isn't so nice, at 40 percent. So, anyone who may have an estate that exceeds these amounts should run, not walk, to their nearest estate planning attorney to discuss options for reducing or even eliminating this tax exposure by more complex estate planning techniques.)

---

* These numbers are in effect as of 2013 and will be indexed for inflation in subsequent years.

However, many couples overlook the state estate tax that may apply to their situation. Not every state has a state estate tax, but those that do often have an estate tax that kicks in at a much lower level. For example, Massachusetts, New York, and the District of Columbia—three jurisdictions in which this author is admitted to practice law—have estate taxes that kick in once the estate exceeds $1 million. See Table 4.1 below.

Out of the states that do impose their own estate tax, these states DO recognize same-sex marriages:

### TABLE 4.1: RECOGNITION STATES WITH ESTATE TAXES

|  | EXEMPTION AMOUNT | TOP TAX RATE |
|---|---|---|
| Connecticut | $2 million | 12% |
| Delaware | $5.25 million | 16% |
| District of Columbia | $1 million | 16% |
| Maine | $2 million | 12% |
| Maryland | $1 million | 16%* |
| Massachusetts | $1 million | 16% |
| Minnesota | $1 million | 16% |
| New Jersey** | $675,000 | 16% |
| New York | $1 million | 16% |
| Rhode Island | $910,725 | 16% |
| Vermont | $2.75 million | 16% |
| Washington | $2 million | 19% |

* This rate may be misleading since the calculation is graduated. For example, the effective rate on the first $100,000 is 39 percent. Other states may have similar graduated calculations, so these rates are the maximum that would be applied.

** While New Jersey does not recognize same-sex marriage, under current law, it treats same-sex marriages from other states as civil unions under its own law.

Out of the states that do impose their own estate tax, these states DO NOT recognize same-sex marriages:

TABLE 4.2: NON-RECOGNITION STATES WITH ESTATE TAXES

|  | EXEMPTION AMOUNT | TOP TAX RATE |
|---|---|---|
| Hawaii | $5.25 million | 16% |
| Illinois | $4 million | 16% |
| Oregon | $1 million | 16% |
| Tennessee (scheduled to change) | $1.25 million | 9.5% |

While $1 million dollars seems like a great deal of money, and people often don't think their estate can reach this level, be careful. I'm not talking only about the money in your checking and savings accounts. Your estate includes all of the value of everything you own at the time of your death: equity in your home; retirement accounts; and the least under-stood and often forgotten asset class: life insurance. Life insurance is often thought of as "non-taxable," because the proceeds of life insurance are not taxable to the beneficiaries. The value, however, of the total death benefit of a life insurance policy is included in the decedent's gross estate for this estate tax calculation. So, if you have life insurance—even through work, as a multiple of your base salary—your total estate could trigger this state estate tax problem.

What can be done about this? Well, getting married, believe it or not, is the simplest answer. States that have a state estate tax and would rec-ognize your marriage allow an unlimited marital deduction for a surviving spouse. We refer to this in our practice as the "Melinda Gates exemption." That is, any spouse can leave another spouse any amount of money and not be subject to state or federal estate taxes.* If the combined estates exceed these trigger amounts, eventually, after both spouses are gone, there could

* The only exception to this general rule is for non-citizen spouses where it does not apply unless certain trusts are established, commonly referred to as Qualified Domestic Trusts (or "QDOTs") for the surviving non-citizen spouse.

be an estate tax for the ultimate beneficiaries of these estates. But, again, a knowledgeable estate planning attorney can help plan to reduce or eliminate these estate taxes.

Gift taxes are another form of transfer tax. They apply when someone transfers wealth to another person.*

Some people may remember that you couldn't transfer more than $10,000/year to anyone without the gift tax (a.k.a. "annual exclusion gifts"). Some may even have been the happy beneficiary of those $10,000 gifts from grandma and grandpa periodically. Well, that number has been indexed for inflation and is currently at $14,000/year per person and will change over time. What this means is that anyone can give anyone up to that amount in any given year and not be subject to gift taxes. If you are married, you can do something called "split-gifting," which essentially means that a married couple can combine this amount and give anyone up to $28,000/year per person, whether it comes from one or the other spouse. This can be a handy tool for transferring wealth from one generation to another.

In addition to these annual rules, there is a lifetime federal exemption that everyone is allowed to use. This amount used to be $1 million, but it has been "unified" with the estate tax amount, so that it is now $5.25 million (also indexed for inflation). What this means is that—in addition to the annual $14,000/per person/year amount—anyone can give away up to $5.25 million during their lifetime without gift tax consequences. However, beware: Whatever portion of the lifetime exemption amount that is used during a lifetime means there is that much less that can be used at death. (You don't get to double dip.) So, if someone wanted to give the beach house to their kid—worth $2 million—then, at death, they could transfer up to (the balance of) $3.25 million in their estate without being subject to estate taxes. These gifts often happen with real estate and can be tricky. There are issues around cost basis and reporting

---

* Transfer tax rules allow unlimited transfers between spouses—now all spouses (same-sex and otherwise) under sections 1056(a), 2523(a) and 1041 of the Internal Revenue Code of 1986, as amended (the "IRC"). Shifting of assets between unmarried persons is taxable, except for the annual exclusion amounts under section 2503(b) of the IRC, or the exclusions permitted for qualified medical or educational expenses under section 2503(e).

of the gift that requires professional advice, so don't try this at home! Seek advice from a competent estate planning attorney if you are contemplating making lifetime gifts above the annual exclusion amount. Fortunately, now that the Supreme Court has ruled in the *Windsor* case, there can be no gift taxes between lawfully-married spouses—same-sex or otherwise. Stated another way, there is an unlimited ability to give property and assets to a spouse without being subject to a transfer tax.

Finally, generation-skipping transfer taxes are similar to estate taxes in that they apply when estates pass to grandchildren or those deemed to be of a generation below the next (the Internal Revenue Code tells us that includes people more than 37.5 years younger than the testator.) The intricacies of how this tax works is beyond the scope of what can be covered here, but here are a few important things: the exemption amounts are the same as the estate tax amounts, so it only applies when a transfer would exceed the $5.25 million amount (from one estate) or above $10.5 million combined from a married couple's estate. Again, anyone with this (very nice problem) should seek advice from an estate planning attorney.

## Social Security, Including Retirement, Disability, and SSDI

The Social Security Administration (SSA) manages a host of benefit plans that all Americans share. Many of these are tied to marital status, and when the really awful things happen in a family, like disability or death, these benefits become essential. Right now, the law that applies to all Social Security benefits for same-sex spouses is that the marriage has to be recognized in the state law of domicile at the time of application for the benefit. What the law actually says is that you can be eligible if you could, under the state law where you live, inherit property from your spouse without a will as would a "wife, husband, widow or widower." If that is the case, then you are eligible for all Social Security spousal benefits.[4] This is what seems to be requiring the SSA to apply the "place of domicile" rule for now.

We are awaiting further guidance from the SSA, but, unless this law is changed or also declared unconstitutional, place of domicile will likely be the rule for all Social Security benefits that derive from being married. The big one, of course, is survivor benefits on Social Security retirement, which may or may not be useful, depending on who in the couple was the higher wage earner and how long (and how much) was paid into the system. For a more comprehensive treatment of how to calculate these benefits, check out the SSA's website at:

SSA's "Retirement Planner: Benefits for You as a Spouse," www.socialsecurity.gov/retire2/applying6.htm[5]

Interestingly, this not only has the effect of allowing Social Security spousal benefits, such as spousal retirement, disability and lump sum death payments, for example, to be available only to same-sex couples in recognition states. But, unlike the other federal benefits that seem not to apply to domestic partners or couples of registered civil unions, here, if those laws include inheritance rights—as most do—then these Social Security benefits may extend to same-sex couples with other quasi-marriage status (namely, civil unions or registered domestic partnerships). Again, we are awaiting further guidance from the SSA on this very point.

While opposite-sex married couples have long enjoyed Social Security spousal benefits at retirement, when disabled, and at one spouse's death, same-sex couples now receive equal access to those benefits, as long as they live in a recognition state. Social Security benefits hinge on the couple's place of domicile—meaning that the state in which they live determines whether the marriage is recognized or not. These benefits include:

## Retirement Spousal Benefit

If you and your spouse live in a recognition state at the time of application, you would be considered eligible for a spousal retirement benefit, as long as other standard Social Security criteria are met. This Social Security benefit is for non-earning or lower-earning spouses, entitling them to collect 50 percent of their spouse's Social Security benefit when they retire. You are only eligible for this payout when your spouse retires AND if your Social Security benefit is less than half of your retired spouse's benefit. If you have already started collecting, your benefit will not change when your spouse retires.

To qualify for such benefits, your spouse would need to have worked for forty quarters and paid into the Social Security system. His or her five highest grossing years are then taken to determine the monthly Social Security benefit. To qualify for the spousal benefit, you would need to have been married for at least twelve months before applying for benefits and be at least sixty-two years old.

If you divorce, you may still be eligible for benefits based on your spouse's status, as long as you have not remarried before age sixty, or age fifty if you are disabled and were married for at least 10 years before the divorce.

### Disability Spousal Benefit

Along the same lines as the retirement benefit, spouses who become disabled with a medical condition expected to last one year or result in death, are entitled to a disability benefit. At the same time, the disabled party's spouse is also entitled to a benefit of up to 50 percent of the worker's benefit.

### Surviving Spouse Benefit

When a spouse dies, the surviving spouse is allowed to continue collecting his or her own benefit, or to collect the full payment of the deceased spouse. The surviving spouse can also collect on their spouse's benefit in order to delay applying for their own benefit, which can increase the ultimate value.

This benefit is available to married couples based on the wage earning spouse's primary residence at death; recognition states acknowledge same-sex spouses to collect this benefit, while non-recognition do not. You must also have been married at least nine months before your spouse's death to qualify. Age-wise, you must be at least sixty, or at least age fifty and disabled. If you are caring for your spouse's child, who is under age sixteen or disabled, you may also qualify for this benefit.

## Supplemental Security Income for Aged, Blind, and Disabled (SSI)

While marrying often carries with it additional Social Security benefits, SSI benefits are the exception. These benefits are generally more difficult to qualify for if you are married and living together. That is because married couples over age sixty-five who are living together must apply for SSI benefits as a couple. The limit on the amount of resources a couple is permitted to have and still qualify is 50 percent higher than for an individual, which makes it very difficult for couples to qualify.

Even if only one spouse meets the age or disability standard, if the married couple lives together, that spouse must apply as an individual, but the income and resources of both spouses are considered. Again, few couples qualify.

On the other hand, if a married couple lives apart, perhaps due to nursing care or otherwise, they will be treated the same as an unmarried couple.

## Applying for Benefits

The process of applying for these benefits (and the scope of benefits available) are well beyond the scope of what can be covered here. There are countless resources on the web for people wanting to understand what benefit programs are out there and how to apply. The advocacy groups who do terrific work in this area have combined resources to produce a series of fact sheets in a series entitled: "After DOMA: What it Means for You." They are helpful and practical and seem to be regularly updated. One example is the one for Social Security Spousal and Family Protections. They can all be found on the HRC website (www.hrc.org) under the marriage tab. Here is the link to this one in particular:

www.hrc.org/files/assets/resources/Post-DOMA_FSS_
Social-Security_v3.pdf

What is important for same-sex couples to remember is that in order to be eligible for spousal benefits, two things need to occur. First, you need to be lawfully married (somewhere)* and, second, you need to

---

* Not only is marriage required for many Social Security benefits, but often the duration of the marriage is a relevant factor for eligibility. For example, for spousal death benefits, the couple needs to have been married for at least nine months prior to death—a rule that was enacted to avoid "death bed" weddings in nursing homes. There is also a rule requiring marriage for at least ten years, if there is a subsequent divorce, again to gain access to spousal benefits at death.

reside in a jurisdiction that recognizes your marriage at the time you apply for benefits. I believe, over time, that this may change, as there are likely to be either new rules from the Social Security Administration on these points, or new court cases challenging this rule, including, perhaps, another case before the U.S. Supreme Court on the question of whether this rule violates the equal protection and due processes clauses of our Constitution. Stay tuned . . .

The issue of a marriage being recognized by a state that would not permit such marriages is not new. There is a large body of case law out there on these questions, mostly from the days when some states allowed inter-racial marriage and others did not. The resolution of this issue involves a complex analysis of "conflict-of-law" issues, which lawyers and professors love to debate.[6] The salient thing to know here is that it is not cut and dry. Some states that do not allow same-sex marriage (a "non-recognition" state) may chose to recognize another state's same-sex marriage for certain purposes, or all purposes (e.g., inheritance rights or divorce.) These are the states that I have referred to as hybrid non-recognition states. The state of the law in this area is very much in a flux and changing almost daily with new cases. For a list of these hybrid non-recognition states see Table A.1 in Appendix A.

Another important thing to remember, in addition to needing to be married, is that you need to actually apply for benefits. Even if they are not currently available to you because you live in a non-recognition state, I advise clients to apply anyway. Application has the effect of tolling the statute of limitations so that, if the rules change, there is a possibility for retroactive benefits to be made available from the date of application. However, this is a tricky area and you should consult with a competent attorney who specializes in it before taking action.

## Private Pension/Retirement Plans and Other Employer Benefit Plans

The Employee Retirement Income Security Act (ERISA) is the federal law that governs the area of retirement and other "qualified" plans sponsored by employers. It is complex. The Department of Labor (DOL) also regulates employer benefit plans, such as health insurance, Family Leave

Medical Act, COBRA, and others. On September 18, 2013, DOL issued guidance about all employee benefit plans and the definition of "spouse" in light of the *Windsor* decision.[7] Similar to the IRS ruling, DOL adopted the place of celebration rule and stated that the term "spouse," where used in all of its regulations pertaining to employee benefit plans, shall include same-sex spouses, even if the employee is domiciled in a state that does not recognize the marriage. This, too, was a huge victory for advocates of equal marriage and could possibly have broader ramifications for many same-sex couples than the IRS ruling when it comes to the couple's financial and retirement planning.[8]

Before *Windsor*, any employer who included same-sex spouses in these plans for any number of purposes would have made those plans "disqualified" for certain employer tax benefits under federal law. Since *Windsor* (and more notably, since the IRS issued its revenue ruling in August 2013[9] and the DOL ruling in September 2013[10]) there are now a whole bunch of employee benefit plans that become available to all same-sex married couples irrespective of where they live. These include:

- Cafeteria Plans (for pre-tax premium payments)
- Health Flexible Spending Accounts (FSA)
- Health Savings Accounts (HSA)
- Health Reimbursement Arrangements
- Dependent Care Flexible Spending Accounts (FSA)
- All retirement, pension and "qualified" plans, such as 401(k) and deferred compensation
- Certain IRA and annuity plans for retirement

Not every employer offers all of these benefit plans, so you'll need to check with your human resources representative at work to find out if yours does, but, if it does—your same-sex spouse is now eligible to participate. The administration of these, however, is tricky, since you can usually only make a change once a year during an "open enrollment" period, or if there has been a change in life circumstances, such as getting married. For those who get married (going forward)—no problem. For those already married—you'll either need to wait until the next open enrollment period, or ask your employer to consider opening a special "window" based on these changes in the law. Indeed, the federal government did just that following the *Windsor* decision by allowing all federal employees to make a host of different elections for the two months following the decision. Each employer may decide to do this differently.

On the con side of this equation, it is important to note that some of the plans, like a Dependent Care FSA or Health Savings Account that are available to same-sex married couples—including the limitations about what a couple can put in—are generally worth less together as a married couple than each person could have done separately. For example, same-sex couples are now (as of September 2013) subject to a $5,000 combined spousal maximum contribution limit for Dependent Care FSA and a $6,450 combined spousal limit for family coverage with Health Spending Accounts. If the same-sex spouse has FSA or HRA coverage from their same-sex spouse, they will be disqualified from making or receiving HSA contributions from their own employer.

Another federally regulated benefit plan that is affected (positively) by *Windsor* is COBRA, which stands for Consolidated Omnibus Budget Reconciliation Act and is used whenever employees are terminated from employment. This important federal law provides protections to newly unemployed workers by guaranteeing that they can continue medical insurance coverage (under certain conditions, notably that they pay all costs) for some period of time, usually eighteen months. (This is also relevant in two other important scenarios: First, for families where there is a sudden death, since that can have the effect of terminating employment as well; this law ensures the family can at least continue the same medical/health insurance coverage for the same period of time. Second, is in the case of divorce. A divorced spouse who is essentially kicked off their former spouse's plan will now have the right to continue coverage, again, so long as they pay for it.

Under DOMA, employers were not required to extend COBRA benefits to same-sex spouses; now they must.

In addition to these items, one of the most important benefits now of being married is that your spouse can't give away his or her retirement plan assets at death to anyone other than you (the spouse) without your written consent. All "qualified" retirement plans will now fall under this rule that has existed for some time for opposite sex spouses. Essentially, when beneficiary forms are completed that designate where the plan assets are to be paid (or sometimes rolled over) at death, they will be presumed to go to the spouse (if the form is not filled out) and can only, if married, no matter where the couple resides, go to a non-spouse with the spouse's written consent. This is sometimes intended, for example, when one spouse has children from a prior marriage that s/he wants to provide for, but again, your same-sex spouse must consent. Any designations that don't meet this standard will not be valid.

What will be interesting to watch is what happens to those existing beneficiary designations if someone has died and can't now change, or who can't get his or her spouse to consent. So far, there has been at least one federal case on this matter out of Pennsylvania, a non-recognition state. Here, a dying woman (married in Canada in 2006 to another woman) somehow was persuaded to change her beneficiary designation for a qualified profit sharing plan from her spouse to her parents, apparently the day before she died.[11] Since her spouse did not consent to this change of beneficiary for this federally governed plan, the judge ruled in favor of the surviving spouse and ordered the annuity payments to be made to the spouse.*

Finally, the other good news to come out of the *Windsor* case and the IRS and DOL rulings is that all pension, 401(k) and other qualified retirement plans that provide benefits for a spouse must now apply that offer to same-sex spouses. Examples of some of these include:

- Surviving spouse annuity payment options;
- Hardship withdrawals for certain expenses like medical, education, and funeral;

---

* There are some problems with this case since the judge, contrary to the subsequent IRS rules, relied on state law that provided that civil unions should have the same benefits as marriage. The IRS has said that all federal tax treatment will extend only to same-sex married people and not to those in civil unions or domestic partnerships. In this case, the judge could not have known this since the IRS regulations were not out at the time of his decision. He also applied a place of domicile rule in his decision and may, with the benefit of the IRS guidance, have been more comfortable applying the place of celebration rule.

- Assignment to an ex-spouse for all or part of the plan assets without triggering any adverse income tax affects;

- Required minimum distribution (RMD) rules are more liberal when beneficiary is a spouse more than ten years younger;

- Spousal consent may now be required to take out loans against these plan assets;

- Attribution rules: A spouse will now be deemed to own stock held in plans for employees. This will be relevant and could change certain SEC disclosure obligations about these stock holdings.

As a result of these changes, many employers may be faced with needing to amend their plan documents to conform with these new requirements. Although the IRS has announced that all qualified retirement plans must comply with these rules effective September 16, 2013, it would appear they are going to give employers some breathing room to make their internal changes. But, keep in mind that guidance on that was still pending at the time of this writing.

The retroactive effect of all this remains to be sorted out. Whether, for instance, with existing plans that are already in pay-out mode, you can now add a spousal survivor option—stay tuned. I am not so sure we can "put the genie back in the bottle" on that one.

What is important to know and remember for same-sex couples in this important area of qualified retirement plans is the following:

1. Beneficiary designation forms matter. Even if you filled them out listing each other as the beneficiary long ago, it may be important to update them if you have become married in the interim. Under federal law, a spouse needs to consent to a beneficiary designation form that attempts to list anyone other than the spouse as the 100 percent beneficiary. Before *Windsor*, same-sex couples were not recognized federally as spouses, and, therefore, were not systematically asked by their employer's human resource departments to sign these spousal consents. Now they should. There is at least one legal theory that says they should have been all along, so go back

and check all beneficiary designation forms for all accounts, plans, and benefits to ensure that you have named the right person. If you have named anyone other than your spouse for any portion of your beneficiary designation, make sure to get your spouse to sign the spousal consent. Remember too, if there is a divorce, don't forget to change the beneficiary designation forms to take your spouse off the form as a beneficiary. Typically, this will all be part of the divorce order or agreement, but sometimes it is missed.

2.  Retroactive benefits may be available. With pension plans, there is usually a one-time election to select the type of annuity payment you wish to receive. Typically, your monthly payment is higher when you elect to receive no spousal benefit after you are gone and slightly less if you want payments to continue if you die before your spouse. In the past, most plans did not recognize same-sex spouses and, therefore, you may have been unable to elect the surviving spouse option. Now you can. And, if it has already been done, you may be able to have a "do-over" on it. At least one federal court in Pennsylvania has said so (at the time of this writing) and others will likely follow suit. We are awaiting regulations in this area from the Department of Labor.

3.  Health insurance and other benefits. With the implementation of the Patient Protection and Affordable Care Act ("Obama-care")[12] this is an area in flux. It is complex. What is important to know for same-sex couples is that the world just changed with the fall of Section 3 of DOMA, and now many married same-sex couples should and will have available to them certain federally regulated employer benefits, such as spousal health insurance coverage, that were not universally available before. We don't yet know whether this will be an area that is based on place of celebration or place of domicile in terms of the marriage from a federal regulation standpoint. What we do know is that the federal government and many other employers may voluntarily choose (as the federal government has done) to make it available to all same-sex married couples, regardless of domicile, thereby applying the place of celebration rule.

In order to have these benefits actually become available, certain choices need to be made on a variety of company or insurance company forms. Typically this is done at the time of new employment, and then once a year thereafter during the "open enrollment" window. Many employers, including the federal government, have opened a special "open enrollment" period for married same-sex couples to re-do their employee benefit selections. This includes not only selection of who can be the beneficiary of your retirement plans, but whether you want your spouse on your benefit plans as a spouse for the range of issues, including health care benefits, Flexible Spending Accounts, etc. In fact, in doing research for this book, I came across an interesting recommended announcement for all employers to use to comply with the state of the new law post-*Windsor*:

### Sample Message to All Employees:

> On June 26, the United Sates Supreme Court announced that a section of the Defense of Marriage Act was unconstitutional. The consequence of this decision is that the spouses and children of an employee in a same-sex marriage may now be allowed to access coverage under some of our employee benefit plans, as well as enjoy some additional federal protections under COBRA and FMLA, for example. Conversely, a same-sex-married employee may wish to leave their current benefit plan and join their spouse's benefit plan with another employer. If you are in a same-sex marriage, please feel free to contact the Human Resources department to review your current benefit elections in the event you wish to add your same-sex spouse. We will allow a limited special open enrollment period from (DATE) to (DATE) in order to allow employees in same-sex marriages to revisit their benefit elections consistent with the guidance above. [13]

So, if your employer has opened the window for you to revisit your employer-sponsored plan benefit elections—do it! Consider the consequences for you and your partner and run the numbers. Often it is less expensive for you to be on one or the other's plan than for each to be on your own respective employer's plan. Consult your financial advisor. A helpful HR professional can also usually walk you through the choices and cost/benefit analysis.

If your employer has not opened a window, ask them to do so. Some professionals who have looked at this believe that a company not opening a window for same-sex spouses to enroll in benefits now violates the Supreme Court decision and could cause the employer to be liable. If you are in that situation and are not able to make headway with your employer, contact one of the advocacy groups listed in Appendix B. These groups often can be helpful in persuading (including suing) the employer to do the right thing.

Finally, the last thing to say about all employee benefit plans, and I have already stated this earlier, but want to reiterate it again here is that **beneficiary designation forms do matter.** Whether you are married or not, please fill them out taking into consideration your partner or spouse. And, if your relationship changes—change the forms.

Sadly, without marriage, same-sex partners can continue to be left out when the horrible things happen, like for Florida Detective Mickie Masburn, whose life partner of eleven years, Lois Marrero, a Tampa police officer, was killed in the line of duty during a bank robbery in 2001. Not only had Lois neglected to name Mickie as the beneficiary of her death benefits at work, but, without marriage and the recognition of being a legal spouse, Mickie was unable to receive one-half of Lois' salary for life. Mickie did petition the Tampa pension board for relief, but was denied in a 7-1 vote. The death benefit was awarded to Lois' blood relatives instead. [14]

## Federal Employee Benefits

The federal government employed more than 4 million people[15] around the country and across the globe in 2011. It would be difficult to have an employee in one state be eligible for certain benefits, like healthcare for their same-sex spouse, but then have it taken away if the employee needed to transfer (for his or her job) to another state that happens not to recognize their marriage. Therefore, the federal government has decided to apply the place of celebration rule to federal employee benefits. This means that the government will make available all such benefits to all same-sex married couples who are lawfully married (when the marriage was entered into), regardless of where they live at the time of receiving benefits.

In short, on the "whether-to-wed" list, if you are a federal employee, there are a host of spousal benefits that would flow if you were married, and none if not. They include:

- Federal Retirement Thrift Savings Plan (FRTSP)
- Federal Employees Health Benefits Program (FEHB)
- Federal Employees Group Life Insurance (FEGLI)
- Federal Employees Dental and Vision Program (FEDVIP)
- Federal Long-Term Care Insurance Program (FLTCIP)
- Federal Flexible Spending Accounts (FSAFEDS) [16]

The Federal Office of Personnel Management has announced that already-retired federal workers who may have made certain elections with respect to their retirement plans can now revisit those choices as a result of the *Windsor* case and recognition of their same-sex spouse. They have two years from the date of that decision to make changes to their retirement benefit elections. So, anyone in this category should consult with their financial planner to determine what makes the most sense for them. Then they should mark their calendars to get new elections submitted for federal retirement plans by June 26, 2015!

Additionally, the Federal Office of Personnel Management announced a new open enrollment period for two months—from June 26 to August 26, 2013 to make new elections with respect to current employee benefits, such as healthcare coverage for spouses, access to Flexible Spending Accounts, etc. If you missed that window, there will be an open enrollment period annually. Check with your personnel office for those dates.

A number of other agencies who manage these benefit plans have made similar moves. For example, the Federal Retirement Thrift Investment Board revised its regulations on September 20, 2013 to include all married same-sex couples in the program's retirement benefits in light of the *Windsor* case, irrespective of which state the employee (or retiree) lives in, so long as they are married.[17] I expect other conforming regulations will be forthcoming.

## IRA Rollover

We sometimes refer to the beauty of tax-deferred income growth as the "eighth wonder of the world." We all know by now that qualified retirement plans generally grow tax-deferred. That is to say, whatever our retirement accounts, such as IRAs or 401(k) plans, may be invested in, they are not subject to income tax on any appreciation in the year the growth or income occurred. Only when you start to withdraw from these plans do you need to declare the withdrawn amounts as part of your ordinary income and pay taxes on them. Some people defer withdrawing from these accounts until they absolutely have to, which, under current law, means when you turn seventy-and-a-half years old. Even then, the amount you need to withdraw is based on a schedule, published by the IRS—commonly known as your "Required Minimum Distributions," or RMD. See the IRS website for instructions and help calculating your own:

www.irs.gov/Retirement-Plans/Plan-Participant,-Employee/
Retirement-Topics---Required-Minimum-Distributions-%28RMDs%29

If you die without having used up or taken out all of the money in one of these retirement accounts, they generally pass to a surviving spouse. Assuming the spouse is the sole 100 percent beneficiary, that spouse has a one-time election that s/he can make, by September 15 of the year following the year of the death, to either "roll-it-over" or pay it out. If the spouse chooses to pay out their deceased spouse's retirement benefit plan, they may get hit with a big tax bill the following year, as that is considered a taxable distribution. However, if they "roll-it-over" to their own retirement account, they can essentially stretch it out for their own lifetime, becoming subject again to the same rules of requiring a RMD by age seventy-and-a-half.

By electing to roll-over an IRA from a deceased spouse, you enjoy the benefit of continued tax deferred compounding on the growth of the assets in that account. A good financial planner can model out what this could mean for your own retirement. This is a big plus to being married for these types of accounts.

## Military Personnel and Veteran's Benefits

There are a variety of spousal benefits for military personnel, from the mundane, such as shopping privileges on the base commissary, to the profound, such as burial rights in a veteran's cemetery. Other benefits include family separation allowance for those deployed; housing allowances for married couples and, of course, medical and retirement benefits for spouses. For a more comprehensive list of spousal and family benefits for military personnel, see the Spouse and Family Benefit Resources on www.miltary.com found at: www.military.com/NewContent/1,13190,Spouse,00.html

All of these now apply for same-sex married couples—regardless of domicile. Even before the *Windsor* case was decided by the Supreme Court, Secretary of Defense Leon Panetta announced at the time of repeal of the "Don't Ask; Don't Tell" policy in 2011 that he was committed to reviewing benefits that had not previously been available to same-sex partners based on existing law and policy. Panetta was quoted saying, "It is a matter of fundamental equity that we provide similar benefits to all of those men and women in uniform who serve their country ..."[18] The Defense Department began working to implement this as a policy system-wide. I can't help but editorialize how far the Department of Defense has come from the "Don't Ask; Don't Tell" policy, which was in place since 1993 and formally repealed on September 20, 2011 by President Obama, to this progressive implementation of marriage benefits for all who serve our country. Bravo!

So, it was not surprising therefore, that after *Windsor,* on August 14, 2013, the Department of Defense announced it will make all spousal and family benefits related to marriage to all same-sex couples, provided they produce a valid marriage license, thereby implementing a place of celebration rule for these couples.[19]

Veteran's benefits were a different story initially following *Windsor,* but they now appear to also be available based on the place of celebration rule. Veterans Administration benefits are governed by a statute that, like DOMA, define a spouse as an opposite-sex person. However, on September 4, 2013, U.S. Attorney General Eric Holder announced he had been instructed by President Obama to "take steps to make veteran benefits available to all lawfully married same-sex couples" in light of the decision.

In effect, this meant not enforcing this statute that is still on the books on the theory that it is now unconstitutional under.[20]

VA benefits that stem from marriage include, of course, spousal benefits upon disability or death, and the right to be buried with your spouse in a veteran's cemetery. But there are many more, such as healthcare, educational benefits and home loan assistance. Surviving spouses of active-duty military personnel are also entitled to a death gratuity of $100,000. Where there is no surviving spouse (or the spouse is not recognized), this payment is made to other surviving next-of-kin, such as parents and siblings. For a more comprehensive list of VA benefits available to spouses, see:

| TABLE 4.3: MILITARY BENEFITS FOR MARRIED, SAME-SEX COUPLES | |
|---|---|
| **GI Bill Benefits** | www.gibill.va.gov/benefits/post_911_gibill/transfer_of_benefits.html |
| **Veterans Health Administration Healthcare (CHAMPVA)** | www.va.gov/hac/forbeneficiaries/champva/champva.asp |
| **Dependency and Indemnity Compensation** | benefits.va.gov/COMPENSATION/types-dependency_and_indemnity.asp |
| **Dependent's Educational Assistance Program** | www.gibill.va.gov/benefits/other_programs/dea.html |
| **VA Guaranteed Home Loan Program** | www.benefits.va.gov/homeloans/ |
| **Burial Benefits** | www.cem.va.gov/burial_benefits/ and www.cem.va.gov/cem/burial_benefits/eligible.asp |

## Immigration

The good news is that immigration rights for a U.S. spouse are now available to all lawfully-married same-sex couples, regardless of domicile. They vest immediately upon a lawful marriage in any of the recognition states.

Indeed, only two days after the *Windsor* decision did we begin hearing reports of bi-national same-sex couples already being awarded green card status (lawful permanent resident alien), based on being married to a U.S. citizen.

Married in New York in October 2012, Florida residents Julian Marsh and Traian Popov were the very first same-sex bi-national married couple to be granted green card status.[21] Although their home state of Florida does not recognize their marriage, the federal government does. The pair was happy to have received notification that Popov—a native of Bulgaria—will receive a green card. They were already discussing which country they might move to should it be denied. Fortunately, they and many other bi-national same-sex wedded couples won't need to move.

The Immigration and Customs Enforcement (ICE) agency, which is part of the Department of Homeland Security, has actually been very helpful to same-sex bi-national couples, even before the *Windsor* decision was announced. For the last two years, the agency has kept a list of same-sex couples whose green card petitions were denied, the officials said, anticipating that the Supreme Court would eventually weigh in on DOMA. Those denials are all now being reversed without couples having to present new applications, if no other issues have arisen. Gay couples with no denials, like Marsh and Popov, will move through the system at the same pace as traditional spouses, officials have reported.[22]

However, despite this good news for bi-national same-sex couples— and it is good news—beware, or you could inadvertently mess up if you don't follow proper procedure. Some foreign nationals who enter the U.S. on temporary visa status, such as a student visa, have, as a condition of being granted that visa, made a declaration that they do not intend to remain here permanently. Marriage can confound this, and an immigration attorney should be consulted before getting married if one of the couple is a non-U.S. citizen.

Non-U.S. nationals here on a visa can only adjust their status based on marriage (meaning, get their green card while in the U.S.) if they entered the U.S. on a visa of some sort. People who enter illegally would have to get their green card outside the U.S. If someone enters the U.S. on a J-1 training visa and is subject to the two-year residency requirement, they may need to return home for two years prior to getting a new status in the U.S., including from marriage. If someone applies for their green card and needs to leave the U.S. and return, they may lose their current status and have to re-enter as a parolee (a form of authorized stay in the U.S. that does not grant any inherent benefits, but allows the person to return to the U.S. and remain until their green card is approved). This is a tricky area. Please consult a qualified immigration attorney for proper advice. There *is* a way to do this right. Depending on the person's visa status, it may become necessary to return home for a brief period and seek a different type of visa in order to return to become married. It is all doable, but can be tricky.

Also, it is important to consider the potential tax implications of changing immigration status. Green cards are subject to expatriation rules on the backend. Giving up a green card should not be an automatic decision.

One final word of caution: Gay and lesbian couples will now be subject to the same rules as straight people in this important area. That is to say, while there is a preference for instant immigration status when one marries a U.S. citizen, it needs to be a real marriage. Those contemplating helping their Russian boyfriend, cute as he may be, to get a green card may get into real trouble if they perpetrate marriage fraud. The Department of Homeland Security, and U.S. Citizenship and Immigration Services take these issues seriously and often asks couples—straight or gay—to prove the bona fides of the marriage in a variety of ways. Marriage fraud cases generally require testimony of friends and family that a valid marriage occurred and the proof that the couple lives together as a married couple. (They really do ask you in separate interviews which side of the bed the other one sleeps on!) Violation of these rules have stark penalties, sometimes criminal, so don't abuse the new privilege we have to gain access to this important benefit.

## Bankruptcy

Bankruptcy is never good news for anyone. It is painful and has long-term implications for one's credit score. If it becomes necessary to file for bankruptcy, married same-sex couples can now file jointly, instead of needing to file separately. The only good news in this is that one set of court filing fees are required, not two.

However, if the couple lives in a state that recognizes its marriage, the bankruptcy court will now apply the tests for assets and income to both people in the married couple, whether or not one or both are filing for bankruptcy protection. The effect of this will be to count the assets and income of both spouses in order to determine whether the one (or both) filing for bankruptcy is eligible for complete liquidation and discharge of the debts (Chapter 7), or whether they can become available for what is known as "reorganization" (Chapter 11), so that a payment plan is essentially worked out for payments to creditors.

The area of debt is a complex one for married couples and can vary rather dramatically depending on what state you live in. For example, couples living in a community property state who are married (and that state recognizes the marriage), will generally be responsible for 50 percent of their spouse's debts. See Table 5.1 for list if community property states. Other, non-community property states generally allow spouses to keep debts separate, so long as the spouse has not co-signed or become a co-obligor or guarantor for the debt. Again, this is a tricky area about which advice from a competent local attorney is prudent.

## What Are the Cons of Getting Married?

While there are plenty of benefits to same-sex couples being married, there are obligations related to marriage that may create some downsides that should also be pointed out, lest you think marriage is a win-win proposition 100 percent of the time. The biggest disadvantages that accompany marriage include:

## Income Taxes

I mentioned earlier the "marriage penalty" that can arise for some regarding income taxes. If this is the case for you, then only you can decide whether that is the factor that tips the scale for you against marriage. I would only caution you to give weighted importance to *all* of the factors outlined in this book before making your final decision.

As a practical matter, there is another con to getting married—even if you aren't caught by the marriage penalty. It has to do with filing requirements. Only those filing from a recognition state can easily, like their straight counterparts, now fill out two income tax forms—a state and federal income tax declaration, typically federal Form 1040 and the state equivalent—as a married couple. But, if you reside in a non-recognition state where state income tax filings are due—fasten your seatbelt, because you may become dizzy trying to understand the complexities that may now be involved in filing your annual income tax returns. Since most state returns are populated from information provided on a federal return, married couples in non-recognition states will likely have to prepare five (yes, FIVE!) separate versions of their tax returns before filing a total of three for the two people involved. Here's how it works:

1. Federal (married) is the first return that will be prepared, and this one will actually be filed.

2. Then, you each will need to do a "dummy" (some say "pro-forma") federal return as a single person, to generate the information needed for your state (single) return.

3. You then each need to prepare separate (single) state returns, which are also filed.

And, if that's not enough, you may (in consultation with your local tax advisor) choose to file a protest that the single state returns they are making you file are unlawful, so as to preserve your rights to potentially amend them later. This would be important if your state changes its mind and soon recognizes your marriage—or, more likely, the Supreme Court finally answers the question of whether there is a federal constitutional right for all same-sex couples to be married. Some have referred to this as the "Full Employment Act for Accountants." It is yet another reason why the patchwork system is not sustainable for long.

It is important to note that not every non-recognition state's department of revenue has yet issued its guidelines on this issue. But some have.

For example, Kansas tax officials announced on October 4, 2013 that all (married) same-sex couples must file their state income tax returns as if each person were single, even if they file married on their federal returns. In this case, the Kansas Department of Revenue has kindly offered to provide a worksheet in its state instruction booklet for income tax filings to help calculate income, deductions and other data for each taxpayer separately. Only a handful of non-recognition states have issued such regulations (as of this writing) but more are expected before April 15, 2014.

Help is on the way, however. I have it on good authority that the makers of Turbo Tax® at Intuit are already working on an "app" to help same-sex couples in every state not only deal with these difficult filing issues, but also to help with the process to evaluate and amend prior year's returns if a refund will be due. I suspect other tax preparation software companies will address this issue as well, but, frankly, I am not sure. You'll need to check with whomever you use for support to make sure they have integrated the "DOMA-demise" in their filing software.

## Medicaid

Medicaid is the federal health benefit program for indigent people. It provides health care coverage, particularly for nursing home care for elderly, when the person or family cannot afford to pay those costs themselves. This program will become even more important in the future as nursing home costs continue to rise. Between 2008 and 2013, the average cost of private nursing home care rose 24 percent, from $67,527 to $83,950 per year, according to Genworth's 2013 Cost of Care Survey.[23]

One approach to mitigating the costs of nursing home or elder care is to obtain long-term care (LTC) insurance. This can sometimes be expensive, but it can also be a terrific way to protect a couple's assets for their eventual heirs, such as children. Since this, too, is a complex area, I strongly encourage people to work with an honest insurance broker who can help you evaluate the cost/benefit analysis of whether LTC insurance makes sense for you and your family. Often, a recommendation from your attorney, accountant, or financial planner, someone not selling the policy, is a good place to start. The Assistant Secretary for Planning and Evaluation at the U.S.

Department of Health and Human Services put out a fairly comprehensive guide about LTC insurance in June 2012 that I would recommend for those considering this important coverage. It can be found at:

http://aspe.hhs.gov/daltcp/reports/2012/ltcinsRB.pdf

If, however, you don't have LTC insurance when the awful thing happens, and one of you needs nursing home care, then you are faced with the difficult choice of whether to private-pay, and possibly use up all of your assets, or try to become eligible for Medicaid and have the government pay.

Since this program was established to help the most needy in our society, there are strict rules for eligibility. They include an asset test. Since these programs are administered by each state slightly differently, I will not list the rules here for all fifty states. However, I'll use Massachusetts' requirements as an example.

The most relevant portion of these rules for this discussion is that the assets and income of **BOTH SPOUSES** are considered for determining eligibility. Therefore, this is one important area where being married could count against you if your spouse has assets or income that cause you, together, to be above the limits for eligibility of these benefits.[24]

All Medicaid programs are administered by the states, sometimes slightly differently, but they are "means-tested" benefit programs. This means that only those who demonstrate real need are eligible. Each state sets slightly different amounts, so an elder law attorney in your state should be consulted before doing any planning in this area.

In 2013 (these numbers are adjusted each year based on inflation), the nursing home spouse in Massachusetts can have $2,000 in "countable" assets and the well spouse can have $115,920 at the time of the application for MassHealth, which is our state's program to administer the federal Medicaid benefits. One advantage of being married is that married spouses are allowed to transfer assets to each other without penalty. Countable assets do not include the home, personal property, and certain income-producing property, including "Medicaid-compliant" annuities, which name MassHealth as the secondary beneficiary (up to the amount paid by MassHealth) after the spouse, and certain other assets.

It is important to note, however, that with proper planning, you can often protect more assets than the limits noted above for the well spouse using certain strategies that only work for married couples. For instance, in Massachusetts, there is something called a Community Spouse Resource Allowance that can provide certain benefits for the unwell spouse at home or in an assisted living facility, and protect nearly everything for the well spouse. Other strategies are available for planning in this area only if you are married. One example is transferring assets into the well spouse's name and then putting them into short-term Medicaid-compliant annuities for the benefit of the well spouse. But, this is not a "do-it-yourself" project. Don't try this at home! It definitely requires the help of qualified elder law attorneys, and these rules do vary somewhat by state.

There are no income limits for the at-home spouse, and there are essentially no income limits for the nursing-home spouse. All of the nursing-home spouse's income—except for a $72.80 per month personal needs allowance and a minimum monthly needs allowance that is payable to the at-home spouse (currently between $1,939 and $2,898, depending on the needs of the at-home spouse)—is paid directly to the nursing home. The Minimum Monthly Needs Allowance, which allows the healthy spouse to keep a portion of the nursing-home spouse's income, would be one advantage of being married. In certain circumstances, after a fair hearing, the at-home spouse can be allowed to keep even more assets, or receive a larger portion of the nursing home spouse's income, if the at-home spouse can demonstrate exceptional circumstances.

For people close to, but still over these amounts, there are a variety of strategies that can be deployed to help the person become eligible for these benefits. This area of the law is known as elder law, or Medicaid planning. It is complex and tricky, and should only be done with an experienced elder care attorney familiar with the rules in this area for your state.

There are also definite advantages to being married if the spouse needing long-term care is able to remain at home. There are a number of Community MassHealth programs in Massachusetts designed to help people who would otherwise require care in a nursing home remain at home. Other states have similar programs, and sometimes, so does the VA, if you are a veteran or married to one. These programs, which also have income restrictions, do not consider the assets or income of the healthy spouse, so the healthy spouse would in most cases be able to transfer his or her assets to the healthy spouse in order to qualify. On the other hand, MassHealth regulations governing eligibility for these Community MassHealth programs generally prohibit the transfer of assets between non-spouses, making it more difficult for partners who live together without being married to qualify for such programs.

Finally, marriage can help protect the family home when one spouse does receive Medicaid benefits. So long as the well spouse remains living in the home (properly titled to both), there is no lien placed on it by Medicaid for the benefits the non-well spouse receives. If you are not married and own a home, you may not even qualify for the benefits if you have too much equity in it. For example, a single person in Massachusetts whose home equity is valued at $802,000 (as of 2013) or above, would not qualify. There is no such test or limit, however, if you are married and a spouse remains living in the home.

Interestingly, this is also an area where the non-recognition states could become advantageous in that, if you are married but living in a state that does not recognize the marriage, the family attribution rules for income and assets may not apply. Be careful here, however. You could win the battle, but lose the war. If you depend on non-recognition as a way to keep your partner/spouse's assets and income from not being "countable" for these purposes, that will only work so long as the patchwork system stays in place. I have mentioned already in a variety of places that I know of further litigation working its way back up to the Supreme Court to cause every state to, perhaps, recognize same-sex marriage. If we win that battle, then those who did their nursing home cost-planning based on having their marriages not recognized (or even based on moving to a non-recognition state at the time of needing nursing home care), you may lose the war and suddenly become ineligible, perhaps retroactively.

## Family Attribution Rules—Tax Code

The tax code is complex. Among the many complexities is something called the "family attribution rules."[25] These rules were meant to close some "loopholes" for wealthy families who were (with the help of their clever lawyers and accountants) transferring wealth among themselves and not being subject to the gift or estate tax consequences discussed earlier. It is a highly technical area and not appropriate for full discussion here, other than to say this: Either a couple is married (and therefore subject to these restrictions), or they are not. With gay couples in long-term committed relationships who choose not to become married, they may be able to take advantage of some of these techniques that are otherwise not available should they get married.

For a more detailed discussion of how a gay couple could transfer wealth from one to the other as an unmarried partner, see "GRITs for Gays," which was published some time ago by this author.[26]

## Debts and Bankruptcy

The main issue here is where one spouse is a "spendthrift" and the other is not. You may, either by mistake or operation of law, become a co-obligor of your spouse's debts, and that could create a situation where you, too, become insolvent and need to file for bankruptcy protection. Generally, this happens in community property states (see earlier discussion), or when a spouse co-signs for a loan, or provides a guarantee for a loan, of a spouse. The most common mistake in this area is simply applying for credit cards. If the application includes income information about both spouses, and both sign the application, then the credit card company will generally treat the credit application as a joint account. They will then require both people to be responsible for whatever charges are made on the account. So, in cases of joint credit card accounts, beware. It doesn't matter who actually made the purchase. If it is a joint account, you will both be held responsible.

Student loan debt is another area of concern for many people. Essentially, the same rules apply. Assuming the debt was taken out by only one spouse and not guaranteed by the other, it is individual debt and will not be "assumed" by the spouse by operation of the marriage.

## Student Loan Eligibility

If you or your partner is considering applying for student loans to attend college or graduate school, both of your income sources will be considered if you are married.[27] If you are not married, you can apply based on your income alone. In some cases, that may be the difference between qualifying for financial aid and not, especially if your partner has a higher income level. Similarly, if you are married, you and your spouse's income will be "counted" on financial aid forms for your children—even if you have not done a second-parent adoption. This, too, is a tricky area, since many private colleges require full financial disclosure of all adults in the home, irrespective of marital status, so you may or may not be able to avoid this.

We did have one couple in our practice where one of the partners had five children to put through college, and the other, frankly, had more assets and income. This factor became the deciding reason why they chose, at least for the college years, not to get married. They also had separate lawful residences, so it worked vis-à-vis the financial aid forms.[28] Many colleges and universities now require disclosure of assets and income for both adults living together irrespective of marriage status.

And if you are currently paying back student loans, the interest paid is deductible only if you are married and file jointly; if you are married and file separately, the interest paid is not deductible.

## Others

In some instances the following items are covered in the previous discussion. Below is a list of the cons of marriage for certain, miscellaneous federal rules:

1. Limits on contributions to Dependent Care FSAs and Health Savings Accounts. Be careful for the transition year of 2013, since you may have been saving based on the separate limits previously available to each spouse who was, prior to *Windsor*, considered unrelated.

2. Social Security has a program called "Supplemental Security Income" for disabled adults and children who have limited resources in terms of income and assets. If you are married, your spouse's assets are counted for the means tests to determine eligibility.[29]

3. Limits on election contributions now will be combined for married couples at the federal level.

4. Federal disclosure laws around stock ownership will be combined for the Securities and Exchange Act of 1934. This will include married couples who own shares of a public company and are an executive officer, or who are married to one, or a "control" person as defined in the act.

5. Federal disclosure laws, particularly for elected officials, may now apply to same-sex spouses. Similarly, the anti-bribery and other federal laws applicable to gifts made to federal officials, employees or elected officials will now likely apply to same-sex spouses.

# CHAPTER 5

# Whether to Wed: State Law Advantages and Disadvantages

In addition to federal rights and benefits, same-sex couples should also evaluate the pros and cons of marriage from a state law perspective. Generally, the list of state benefits and responsibilities to marriage ONLY applies to couples living in states that recognize same-sex marriage. Some or all of them, however, may apply to same-sex couples who are lawfully married elsewhere if the state recognizes out-of-state same-sex marriages. (These are referred to as "hybrid non-recognition" states, like Oregon, for example.)

## Pros

### Inheritance Laws, Including Spousal Elective Share

Every state has intestacy laws that govern what happens to someone's property (assets) if they die without a will or trust in place. These laws generally prescribe a list of blood relatives, including spouse and children, to inherit. Every state is slightly different; however, in general, someone who dies without a will in place, but who is lawfully married (and that marriage is recognized by the state whose laws apply to the estate), can have their spouse inherit at least half, and often all, of the estate, especially if there are no children.

In addition, as part of these state inheritance laws, there is usually a "spousal elective share" right. The "spousal elective share" right was put in place many years ago by most states to protect a long-term spouse who gets pushed out of the picture in the later years. The classic example of this is the stay-at-home mom who dutifully raises the children and cares for the home, and later learns that the hubby changed his will to leave his entire estate to his mistress. What the spousal election laws say is that a spouse can "elect against the will" and simply take half of everything in the estate, instead of whatever the spouse purported to leave her in his will. It guarantees that at least half of any married person's estate will go to his/her spouse.

This right now vests with all same-sex married couples. The jury is still out on whether this will apply in non-recognition states. As of this writing, it likely will not, except perhaps in hybrid non-recognition states, like Oregon. Therefore, this "benefit" of marriage only applies for couples married and residing in a recognition state who also die in a recognition state. I expect there to be challenges to this limited application, but for now, know that it not only means something in terms of what state you get married in or live in, but also where you die.

Finally, for same-sex married couples who die without a will, the administration of their estates is governed by state law. In recognition states, this will now include a preference for the surviving spouse to essentially (almost automatically) be named as the executor for the estate. (This is called different things in different states, e.g., personal representative.) This is the person legally authorized to take possession of the assets in the estate and distribute them according to the law (again, if there is no will.) The point here is that the same-sex surviving spouse can be in charge of their late spouse's affairs during a wind down process, usually in front of rights that other biological family members might have had, such as parents, siblings, or even children.

The same can be said of making burial or other final arrangements. A surviving spouse (at least in a recognition state) always has priority to make those decisions. The horror stories in this area abound for gay couples.

If you are married but reside in a non-recognition state, it will be important to attempt to deal with this issue by designating an agent responsible for your remains, which, of course, can be your spouse. These legal documents are often a creature of state statute and your local estate lawyer should be able to help you with this as well.

## Spousal Privilege for Testimony

Most states have a basic rule of evidence that spouses are not required to testify against the other spouse in any legal proceedings of any sort, including criminal cases. This is called the "spousal privilege" rule. As of now, same-sex married couples can invoke the spousal privilege law in recognition states, but in non-recognition states, it generally will not apply.[1] However, in addition to recognition states and non-recognition states, there is a third "hybrid" category of non-recognition states that (while not allowing gay marriage to be performed in their state) will recognize out-of-state gay marriages for all state law purposes. In these cases, spousal privilege *would* apply. There is also now some uncertainty about what a federal court would do in a non-recognition state about this issue: Apply spousal privilege or not? It depends, fundamentally on whether a place of celebration, or a place of domicile rule applies, which we think, for now, can be decided by each federal judge, perhaps differently. (This is yet another reason why the Supreme Court will eventually have to weigh in on these issues.) These laws will very likely continue to evolve and change as state laws evolve.[2]

## Tort Claims for Loss of Consortium

A sad reality is that sometimes bad things happen to people, such as tragic car accidents, plane crashes, or even medical malpractice. When these events occur, the law provides a way for victims to claim damages in a court under tort laws. Among those claims for damages are claims for reimbursement of medical expenses, damages for pain and suffering or lost wages, and the like. Another claim is sometimes for "loss of consortium" by a spouse. The key term here, of course, is spouse. Now that same-sex marriage is recognized in many places, a same-sex spouse, in these awful circumstances, can legally make such a claim.

We have the same issues here between recognition and non-recognition states. The claim is clearly available if you bring such an action in a recognition state. It is less clear whether it is/will be available in a non-recognition state, but likely not until the Supreme Court addresses the equal protection and due process issues that arise from this patchwork application of rights.

## Worker's Comp Benefits

Most states provide worker's compensation benefits for injuries, or even death, that happen at work. These benefits are primarily focused on and provide for the injured worker. But, in the event of death, there is often a spousal benefit available. However, you need to be a spouse to be able to make the claim. Therefore, this is now likely only available in recognition states.

## State Estate Tax Spousal Exemption

This is a big one for many. Not every state applies a state estate tax. Many do, however, and when it applies, it is almost always kicks in at a lower threshold than the federal estate tax. For a complete list of states that have a state estate tax, see Table 4.1 and Table 4.2 in Chapter 4. For example, New York, the District of Columbia, and Massachusetts (the three jurisdictions in which this author is admitted to practice law) apply a state estate tax for estates that exceed $1 million.[3] While that even feels like a big number for most people, they often forget what is included in that amount: everything you own at the time of your death, less any obligations owed to other people. So, for instance, the value of your property (or 50 percent of it if jointly held), less the mortgaged amount. All of the value in your retirement, savings, and investment accounts, and here's the one that catches most people off guard: life insurance! These are all part of your estate.

Life insurance is one of the most misunderstood asset classes when it comes to estate taxes. People often think of life insurance as "tax free." It is true that there is no *income tax* payable by the recipient of the proceeds of life insurance. However, the full death benefit amount is included in the gross estate of the decedent for purposes of determining whether this estate tax threshold has been met. So, if someone has some modest retirement and other savings, maybe considerable equity in their home and decent life insurance, even that which you get from work as a multiple of your base salary, oftentimes you can trigger this estate tax threshold.

Why is this important here? Well, if you're married and the state estate tax that would otherwise apply is from a state that recognizes your marriage: it's ZERO! There is an unlimited marital deduction allowed for married couples. There are ways to optimize the amount that can be left to anyone other than a spouse in these states through good trust-based estate planning.

Again, this is an area where it is important to run the numbers. If you live in a state that has a state estate tax and are not married, consult with a competent estate planning attorney to evaluate what the estate tax would be with and without being married. To some great surprises, I have personally run these numbers now for dozens of clients in my office who have been together for decades and who often didn't realize that there was a state estate tax (that becomes due, by the way, within nine months of the date of death, whether the estate is liquid or not). It is not uncommon for my clients, once they realize how much these taxes inflict on the surviving partner, to scurry down the hall to meet our resident Justice of the Peace to fix the problem and get married so that it ceases to be an issue.

## Healthcare Decisions

This area is sometimes the most delicate. It has become common knowledge that, periodically, one's life partner is boxed out of medical decisions, not permitted to speak to the doctors in the event of a tragic accident, and sometimes not allowed to make medical decisions for the other. To address this risk, gay and lesbian couples have for decades now worked to put legal documents in place to address this problem. They include a healthcare proxy or agent appointment, HIPAA release, and sometimes a living will. (These documents are more fully discussed in Chapter 8.) It is still important for same-sex couples to do this work, even if they are married and live in a recognition state, if they ever travel to non-recognition states and/or may move there.

Fortunately, great progress has been made in this area. First, marriage provides instant benefits in this respect. Spouses are allowed, usually under state law, to make medical decisions for one another if the unwell spouse cannot speak for him/herself, have access to medical information, and even make end-of-life decisions. Indeed, in 2010, President Obama directed the Department of Health and Human Services to issue regulations directing hospitals to allow patients to be able to choose their visitors, including same-sex partners. While those regulations became effective in January 2011, bigotry still exists in many parts of our country, and this doesn't always happen automatically.

Certainly in recognition states, it is increasingly easier to be recognized by hospitals and clinicians as "immediate family" when identified as a spouse. But, such is not always the case in many non-recognition states.

## State Property Law Rights

There are a variety of issues that come up with respect to ownership of real estate and marriage. As a general matter, property law is governed by state law. Although certain federal laws come into play (like the federal capital gains taxes that may be due upon the sale of your home), generally, property law is a state issue, and marriage helps better protect property that is jointly owned.

While owning a home together can present a variety of issues, particularly if it was not initially purchased by both people in a couple, here are the property issues that marriage will most directly affect:

1.  Title and Creditor Protection

    There are three ways for a couple to hold title to real estate:

    a.  Tenancy in Common ("TIC")

        This way of holding title allows two or more people to own an "undivided" percentage interest (usually for a couple 50/50, but it can really be whatever percentage you choose) with no rights of survivorship. This is sometimes helpful where the "deal" between a couple is not equal and they want it reflected in the actual ownership instrument. It is also useful when the "deal" is that my share needs to go back to my kids or other family after my death, not my partner or spouse. So, for example, if my husband and I own our beach house as tenants in common 50/50, then, unless I leave my ownership interest to him in my will or trust, he may not necessarily inherit it from me upon death. I am free to leave it in my estate plan documents to others, or even sell my half to others (absent some joint ownership agreement we may have entered into at the outset that prohibits this or gives him a right of first refusal to buy it first), even while we're both alive and owning the property together. This is usually not the best way to hold title with a partner or spouse—unless you've made sure to do your estate plans together and leave each other the other's half (or whatever portion you own) of the property. Interestingly, if you do that, there could be some tax advantages to holding property this way, since, for estate tax purposes, the value of a 50 percent or less ownership interest at death could be discounted for "lack of control" and reduce the value of the estate somewhat. Always consult your estate lawyer (not just your real estate lawyer) before deciding whether this option makes sense for your situation.

b.  Joint Tenants with Rights of Survivorship ("JTWRS")

This is often the most common way that couples in a committed (unmarried) relationship hold title to real estate when, indeed, they want the other one to inherit the interest in the property upon the passing of the first partner. It is, as you will see, essentially the same as the next form or ownership, tenancy by the entirety, in that the co-owner has automatic rights to be the sole owner upon the death of the first owner. There can be some tricky elements, however, if, before the first owner passes away, s/he needs to go into a nursing home and can't afford to pay for it. Then, this asset may become "countable" for purposes of determining eligibility for Medicaid assistance for the nursing home costs, and it may be subject to a lien for those costs paid after that person passes away. (It may not be countable if the unwell spouse intends to return home.) Again, this is tricky stuff. Consult a lawyer specializing in elder or Medicaid law to decide how best to handle this.

c.   Tenants by the Entirety ("T by E")

Finally, tenants by the entirety is the typical way that most married couples hold title to real estate, and is ONLY available if you are married! As of now, it is also only available in recognition states, or in states that recognize out-of-state marriages. Not only does it mean that the surviving spouse will inherit the other's interest in the property at death, but it provides an additional level of creditor protection for both spouse's potential debts during their lifetime. Because the law fuses a married couple's ownership interest into this one thing, if either of them are sued and owe money as a result—say in a malpractice action for a doctor—the creditors cannot force the couple to divide the ownership interest to pay the debts of one person of the couple. It is protected. (There are also "homestead" laws in many states that provide similar protection on your primary residence, usually up to a certain dollar amount. Each of these vary by state, and your local real estate closing attorney can advise you on this at the time of closing.) Homestead protection is usually available for all of the three different types of property ownership—TIC, JTWRS or T by E—but needs to be declared, usually by filing something along with the deed in most states' registry of deeds office.

Another big advantage of holding property as T by E is to protect the value of the home at death, if one person in the married couple needed nursing home care that was paid for by Medicaid. This title feature allows the home to pass to the surviving spouse without the home being subject to any Medicaid recovery at death.

When a couple lives and resides, however, in a recognition state, say New York, but owns a second home in a non-recognition state, say Florida, it is likely that the property ownership records will need to be different. For example, in New York, the couple can (and probably should) hold title to the property as T by E, but in Florida will only be able to do TIC (50/50, for example), or JTWRS, since Florida does not recognize their marriage. The funny thing about this example (which is anything but funny) is that Florida law, I'm told, would require those married people to list themselves as "single" on the Florida deed, since under Florida law, at least today, they are not married. Some people are doing work-arounds, like saying something such as, "Mary Smith, single under Florida law at the time of the filing of this deed, but lawfully married to Sue Jones in and under the laws of New York at the same time." Again, speak to a good lawyer who understands these issues, since you always want to preserve your rights to property from an inheritance perspective, if the law changes after someone (maybe suddenly) passes away.

2.   Trigger "Due on Sale" Clause in Mortgages

There is a federal law called Garn St. Germain, which was enacted to keep mortgage companies and banks at bay when couples needed to change the deeds to their property, either because of marriage or estate planning. Anyone who has ever purchased a home and taken out a mortgage is familiar with the breathtakingly high stack of papers needed to be signed at closing. Among these many forms is one that says something like this: If you change the deed to your house in any way, we reserve the right to "call" your mortgage as due, since we will deem that change in your deed to be a "sale" and, therefore, make your mortgage "due-on-sale." What Garn St. Germain says is that banks and mortgage companies are not permitted to exercise this clause if the reason why the deed was changed was because of marriage, e.g., I wanted to add my new spouse's name to the deed; or if it is because you are putting your house into your trust for estate planning purposes and to avoid probate. There are certain conditions that need to be met for the latter, such as you need to be a trustee and beneficiary of the trust and the owner in possession of the property, among others. So, for those of you who captured the historically low interest rates on mortgages in recent years and don't want to give those up by having your mortgage holder try to accelerate your mortgage and effectively require you to refinance at higher rights: good news. Your marriage won't do that! However, this exemption does not apply to other forms of legally recognized same-sex relationships, such as civil unions and domestic partnerships. So, this is one reason why marriage is better.

3.  Capital Gains Taxes

    Finally, everyone who owns a home hopes, over time, that it appreciates. In fact, most do. And, sometimes, when nearing retirement, couples choose to downsize, or even relocate to a warmer climate. In these instances, there can be a large capital gains tax due upon the sale of the property. Not so long ago, Congress changed the law in this area to allow every individual to keep (without capital gains tax due) the first $250,000 of gain on his or her principal residence—or $500,000 for a married couple. So, simply put, being married gives you more "bandwidth" to realize a gain in your home without it being subject to capital gains tax. (Note: This even extends for up to two years after one spouse dies—yet another advantage of being married!)[4]

## *Family Trust(s) that Provide for Spouse as Beneficiary*

Trusts are contracts, and as such, are governed by state law. Many states have statutes that pertain to trusts and regulate them in a host of ways. While some trusts are living trusts and used primarily to avoid probate, sometimes there are family trusts (or irrevocable trusts) that exist for generations to transfer and preserve wealth.

The important feature here is where a family trust, sometimes called a Dynasty Trust, provides for multiple generations of family members. It sometimes also provides for the spouses of those family members. If it does, and that trust is governed by the law of a state that would recognize your marriage, you're in luck! If it does not, then you may be out of luck. Even if the trust is governed by the laws of a state that does not recognize same-sex marriage (so that the same-sex spouse cannot be a beneficiary but an opposite sex spouses could be), there is a chance you could have the trust "moved" to a friendly jurisdiction where it is then allowed. This is a process known as "decanting." Decanting of trusts is not allowed in every state, and many states have specific laws governing how this can be done. So, again, consult a competent estate attorney if this situation applies to you.

## Cons

Of course, with every list of benefits and reasons to get married, there are other disadvantages that cause couples to stop and think. These are the big reasons, on a state basis, to pause:

### Divorce

While divorce is an ugly word, it's a reality. Studies show that roughly half of all marriages in the U.S. now end in divorce. While there is precious little data on same-sex divorce, I have no reason to believe this population will be immune from the same fate. Indeed, the lead couple in the landmark decision in Massachusetts that gave us our first gay marriage in 2004, Julie and Hillary Goodridge, sadly ended their marriage in divorce after fighting so hard to secure those rights for themselves and others.

The topic is too broad to properly cover here. The main points I want to make about divorce is that it is something everyone who is considering getting married must put on their radar screen as they evaluate the "whether-to-wed" question for themselves. That starts with considering whether a prenuptial contract, or "prenup," is appropriate. Every couple will be different in their personal feelings on this. A prenup it is often indicated when there are disparate assets (meaning one person has considerably more wealth than the other), or when one of the parties may be from a wealthy family and stands to inherit considerable assets that are intended to stay with that side of the family.

As a general matter, prenuptial agreements require certain formalities to be respected when entering into them, in order that they will withstand challenges later on and be considered legally binding. Much to the chagrin of online legal websites, such as LegalZoom.com, this is definitely an area where you can't simply download a form and fill it out. You must go through a certain process for the agreement to be enforceable later on. Generally, that includes each party providing "full and fair" financial disclosure to one another about all assets, liabilities, and income. Typically, each party needs to be represented by separate lawyers, and, often, depending on the rules in your state, the agreement needs to be "fair and reasonable" at the time it is entered into and enforced.

Like marriage, divorce is governed by state law, as are prenuptial (and postnuptial) agreements. For more detailed information about how these things work in your state, consult an expert in the field. This is an area in which the proverbial "ounce of prevention" is truly worth the "pound of cure."

If you live in a non-recognition state, having been lawfully married in a recognition state, divorce can be tricky, or even impossible. Some non-recognition states refuse to take jurisdiction over the marriage for purposes of dissolving it: In other words, you may not be allowed under your home state's laws to get divorced where you live. Elizabeth Schwartz, a Florida lawyer specializing in gay and lesbian issues calls this the "wedlocked" problem. Generally speaking, most states won't allow you to be divorced by their local courts, unless you are a resident there. Residency sometimes requires proof of certain things, including paying local taxes. So, the gay couple from Fort Lauderdale who happily marry in Provincetown, Massachusetts, while on vacation, will have a rude awakening if they try to get divorced in Florida, since courts there won't recognize that marriage for purposes of the divorce. The couple could be forced to return to Massachusetts, establish residency there (i.e., now pay state income taxes where they didn't before, since Florida does not have state income taxes), before they can become divorced there. I call this the "double whammy."

The problems become compounded when children are involved. Some states, for instance, do not recognize "de-facto" parents, that is to say, parents who share equally in primary childcare responsibilities while residing with a child for reasons other than money. In a divorce, the judge will decide custody and visitation rights issues based on what is in the best interest of the children. However, if one of the parents is neither the biological parent or adoptive parent—and the children are in a non-recognition state, that other parent may have no claim for parental rights upon dissolution of the marriage.[5]

Every state is different, so do consult with an expert. California, for instance, identified this problem for same-sex couples married in California who moved elsewhere. The state adopted a law that permits only same-sex couples or registered domestic partners who have moved to a non-recognition state to return to California to dissolve the marriage or partnership under certain criteria. The other states that currently allow divorce for non-resident same-sex couples, provided they are from a state that won't permit them to be divorced, are Delaware, Minnesota and Washington, D.C. Vermont will, as well, provided there are no children involved in the family situation.

Once you find a court to hear your case, the rules, again, will vary. Generally speaking, each state's laws will govern how property is allocated upon divorce, and whether alimony is required to be paid, how much, and for how long. State laws will also decide child custody and visitation rights, if applicable. One interesting question that is as yet unresolved in many states is whether the couple's time together in a committed relationship prior to marriage (since marriage wasn't available for the life of their relationship) should be considered when applying the formulas about splitting assets. Apparently, different courts have gone in different directions on this question.[*] A common misconception is that upon divorce, all property is

---

[*] Mass. Gen, Laws Ch. 208, § 48 provides that a "court may increase the length of the marriage if there is evidence that the parties' economic marital relationship began during their cohabitation period prior to the marriage." In accordance with this statute, a court may, with its power of equity, extend the length of a marriage for purposes of divorce. For same-sex couples, if there is evidence of a longer "economic marital relationship," this power could be important for alimony determinations. For example, in the case of *Russo-Martines v. Martines*, 987 N.E.2d 620, the court determined that the opposite-sex couple's economic marriage lasted twenty years, instead of the five years and nine months that they were legally married.

simply split between the parties 50/50. This is usually not the case—except if your marriage was in (or you lived as a married couple in) a community property state, and then it is only the case for the assets acquired during the marriage.

Prior to DOMA's demise, divorce payments, including the splitting of retirement assets and other division of property by same-sex couples, created big tax problems. Since the federal government didn't recognize the marriage, it therefore wouldn't recognize the divorce. As a result, those payments were taxable under the gift tax rules and not deductible under the income tax rules. However, that is no longer the case. Given the IRS ruling issued in August 2013[6] now all lawfully married spouses will be treated as married wherever they reside, so even if they move to a state that does not recognize their marriage, alimony payments would still be deductible and not subject to gift tax. However, in almost every state that doesn't recognize same-sex marriage, they also don't recognize same-sex divorce, and as mentioned already, may not allow you to become divorced in their state. There are, however, already some exceptions to that rule, such as Illinois and New Mexico.[7]

## Community Property States

While I am neither admitted to practice, nor terribly familiar with, all of the nuances of community property state laws, I do know this—if you get married in (or live in) one of those states, there can be some downsides if it all goes horribly wrong. The biggest issue is the right, generally, of a spouse to "own" one-half of each other's income and assets (acquired during the marriage). Absent a valid prenuptial agreement to the contrary, this can catch many couples by surprise, particularly if they live in one of the community property states that recognizes their marriage, like California or Washington. For a complete list of community property states and identification of those that recognize and don't same-sex marriage, see Table 5.1 below.

There are other complexities for same-sex married couples, identical to those for opposite sex married couples, when it comes to filing income tax returns as well. In community property states, each spouse has a right to an undivided one-half share of any marital income and property.

Essentially, each spouse has to report half of the total community income, as well as half of all community deductions, in addition to his or her separate income and deductions. There are other rules that complicate this basic structure, which may change how it applies to certain assets.

| TABLE 5.1: COMMUNITY PROPERTY STATES |
| --- |

| Non-Recognition |
| --- |
| Arizona |
| Idaho |
| Louisiana |
| Nevada* |
| New Mexico |
| Texas |
| Wisconsin |

| Recognition |
| --- |
| California |
| Washington |

# Neither Fish nor Fowl Category (Meaning Not Sure if It's a Pro or Con):

There are a variety of other legal, tax and/or financial considerations related to marriage that do not fit squarely into a pro or con area, but that I believe, are worthy of mention here:

---

* Although Nevada is not a "recognition state" in the general sense, Nevada same-sex couples in registered domestic partnerships are required to use the community property rules when preparing their income taxes, in accordance with Internal Revenue Service Publication 555. (http://www.irs.gov/publications/p555/ar01.html)

## Life Insurance

Life insurance, regulated by the states (often differently) is an important component to most family's financial plans. The most basic reasons people often put this important financial tool in place is to protect each other and their children, if they have any, in the event of a sudden death—particularly of the primary bread winner in the household. Even when there is not one primary bread winner, but the overall economics of the family depend on both incomes, the sudden loss of one could be devastating. Typically, therefore, life insurance is in place to sometimes cover the following items, in the event that one spouse dies unexpectedly:

1. Pay off a mortgage on the home so that the family can continue to live where they are without disruption or stress;

2. Fund college education plans for dependent children;

3. Provide funds to help pay for family care needs, given the loss of one spouse or parent, which could include housekeepers, cooks, nannies and the like;

4. Sometimes, to have liquidity to pay estate taxes.

With the recent important changes in the law, all of items 1-3 still apply to anyone's analysis when they get married and start a family. The last one may not. The reason for that is what was discussed earlier when I talked about estate taxes. Now that same-sex marriages are recognized for all federal tax purposes, there will never be a federal estate tax upon the passing of the first spouse. Only if the estate is large enough (as of 2013, this means combined between both spouses above $10.5 million), might there be a federal estate tax. If so, oftentimes having life insurance in place to cover that exposure may still make sense. If this nice-to-have problem area is a concern, it is important to remember that there are other advanced estate planning techniques that people can deploy to mitigate or even eliminate the estate tax exposure, so consult a good estate planning lawyer if this applies to you.

However, don't forget about state estate taxes. Again, if you're married and your estate is governed by the law of a recognition state (usually because that is where you were domiciled at the time of your death), then there is no need for life insurance for these purposes, since no estate tax will be due. But, if you are in one of the four states that has a state estate tax and does not recognize same-sex marriage (Hawaii, Illinois, Oregon or Tennessee), you likely may still need to plan for this payment to be made and should get or keep your life insurance for these purposes. See Table 4.1 and Table 4.2.

If you have a fully paid up life insurance policy that was primarily for estate tax coverage reasons that you don't need, you may consider using it for a charitable contribution and get a current income tax deduction for the cash value of the policy. Just a thought . . .

From an employer perspective, life insurance just got a lot more tricky to provide as a benefit. If you are in a recognition state, no problem. But, if you have employees in a non-recognition state you may need to make special arrangements with your insurance provider to be able to include same-sex spouses and/or their children.


## *Medicare*

Medicare is the federal health insurance program designed for senior citizens and those with certain disabilities to assist with the costs of health care. It has four major parts:

**Medicare Part A:** Hospital insurance, covering inpatient stays in hospitals, skilled nursing facilities, and hospice care, and some types of home health care;

**Medicare Part B:** Medical insurance, covering medically necessary doctors' services, outpatient care, medical supplies, and preventive services. (Together, Parts A and B are referred to as "Original Medicare");

**Medicare Part C:** Medicare Advantage Plans, which are private health plans that contract with Medicare to provide both Part A and Part B benefits, as well as, most often, prescription drug coverage;

**Medicare Part D:** Prescription drug coverage added to Original Medicare, as well as to some types of Part C plans with no drug coverage.

Virtually all Americans become eligible for Medicare simply by turning sixty-five years old. Certain aspects of the program, however, do depend on your work history, your access to other health care, your health status, and your income. In some instances, having a spouse alters the way you access these benefits. The best summary of this issue I have seen is a fact sheet published by one of the advocacy groups mentioned earlier:

www.hrc.org/files/assets/resources/Post-DOMA_Medicare_v3.pdf

Essentially, marriage can allow you to use your spouse's qualifying quarters of work, if you do not have enough, to become eligible at least for Part A. In some situations, you can use your former or deceased spouse's qualifying quarters as well. You will, however, need to combine your and your spouse's income to determine your premiums for Parts B and D. So in this case, marriage may not be a good thing.

It is important to note, however, that, like Social Security (right now, at least), these marriage benefits and burdens with respect to Medicare extend only to those in recognition states based on the place of domicile rule that Medicare is forced to follow for now.

### Other Employee Benefits

There are other employee benefits that are not governed by federal laws (like ERISA) that, presumably, would extend to same-sex spouses at least in recognition states, and even in non-recognition states that have employment non-discrimination laws that cover sexual orientation or identity. It is important to note here that there are still no federal laws prohibiting discrimination in the employment context based on sexual orientation.* The late and first ever openly gay congressman, Gerry Studds (D-Massachusetts), was a strong supporter of the Employment Non-Discrimination Act (ENDA) bill to prohibit employment discrimination across the U.S. on the basis of sexual orientation or gender identity.[8] While the proposal includes exemptions for religious organizations and certain other tax-exempt private membership clubs, opposition remains strong. It would appear that the recent debate around including transgender people has stalled, but not foreclosed this important legislation. (Interestingly, a 2008 Gallup poll indicated that 89 percent of those surveyed believed that gay and lesbian people should have "equal rights in terms of job opportunities"). However, unless or until some version of it is passed, everyone needs to be mindful about claims made to employers about benefits—particularly if they are in a non-recognition state that does not have a local (state) anti-discrimination law. They may not be protected if there is backlash, including outright discrimination, by the employer.

## Charitable Planning

This is another area that may be neutral when it comes to the whether to wed question. On one hand, as already mentioned, some charitable planning that was motivated by potential estate tax exposure may have just gone away now that marriage is now recognized by the feds. If, however, your marriage put you (together) in a higher tax bracket (the marriage penalty) from an income tax perspective, you might be more motivated to increase your lifetime charitable giving to reduce the effect of that.

There are, however, at least a few opportunities identified so far where marriage boosts certain charitable planning strategies. One of them is in the area of charitable gift annuities. These are too complex to fully explain here[9], but it is important to note that if you are considering doing

---

*Federal employees in the executive branch are covered by President Clinton's Executive Order from 1998 that prohibits employment discrimination based on sexual orientation. Many states and municipalities have similar local laws, and according to surveys by HRC, a majority of Fortune 500 companies have adopted private corporate policies to prohibit employment discrimination based on sexual orientation, often, but not always, extending to spousal employee benefits.

one of these now, since the "gift" now qualifies for the unlimited federal marital deduction, you can more easily do one of these for both you and your spouse. Another benefit to marriage in the charitable planning area is around charitable remainder trusts, where both people in the married couple can create and contribute property to the CRT freely (whereas previously they could not.)[10] A good resource for professional planners in this area is the Planned Giving Design Center (www.pgdc.com).

## State Income Taxes

There may or may not be a difference between single, married filing jointly, or married filing separately, depending on the state you live in. For example, Massachusetts is basically a flat tax state and, as such, there is rarely a difference in the total tax under the three alternatives. Alternatively, a state such as California that has graduated tax rates based on income, as well as their own version of the alternate minimum tax, can have a dramatic difference in state taxes. It is equally important to review the state tax implications of each filing status when analyzing the federal implications. Don't just look at the federal implications or the state implications—look at everything together.

## International Taxes

From an international tax perspective, it is smart to also consider the implications of changing your marital status. There may be inconsistencies with regard to tax filings that increase or decrease global taxes, as well as tax elections and treaty positions that may be available, depending on your filing status.

# CHAPTER 6

# As We Move or Travel around These United States

As previously mentioned, there are now two categories of states with respect to availability of equal marriage rights for same-sex couples: recognition and non-recognition states. There is perhaps a third category that is the one to watch as the most interesting. This is the category where the state does not provide equal marriage rights, but will recognize a marriage performed in a recognition state sometimes for all purposes, and other times for only limited purposes. I have called this category the hybrid non-recognition states. To add even more complexities, some states will recognize some of the other legal status of same-sex couples, even where they don't offer it—such as civil unions and domestic partners. And, it changes frequently, which is why I do not here summarize the state of the states in this regard. See Appendix A for a state-by-state analysis of laws on same-sex marriage at the time of this writing; and see the web resources in Appendix B for more up-to-date information about this issue of cross-border recognition. Included in Appendix A is a table (Table A.1) that summarizes this third category of "hybrid non-recognition" states that nonetheless recognize out-of-state same-sex marriages. The most recent of which to be added was Oregon on October 16, 2013.[1]

This leads to what many have referred to as the "patchwork" effect of laws around the country. The example previously given is the most poignant one for me: My husband and I were married in the Commonwealth of Massachusetts on September 1, 2007. From that date, at least in Massachusetts, we were afforded all of the same rights and privileges given opposite-sex married couples in the state under state law, but none of those from the federal government under federal law. Post-*Windsor*, we now enjoy all federal rights, benefits and responsibilities, as well as state benefits and obligations, so long as we continue to reside in Massachusetts (and die here).

But, what if we someday decide to retire to sunny Florida? Are we still married if we move there? Today, our marriage would not be recognized for all state law purposes but would be for (many, but not all) federal law purposes. Again, the issue of recognition is confusing since out-of-state marriages that would not be lawful in another state may or may not be recognized for some or all purposes depending on how that state's conflict of law principles are applied by its courts.[2]

The reality is still unfolding and changing. Remember the couple in the preface of the book from Ohio? They hired the medical transport plane to take them to Maryland to be married, and then returned home to Ohio. A judge there has ordered their local clerk to list them as married on the death certificate. Will this then require the state to recognize them as married for any benefits that flow from that? Truth is, we don't know yet. So, what is the solution? Some say, "Marry early and often!" While there is debate in the law about whether someone who is indeed already lawfully married somewhere can (legally) get married again, that is precisely the strategy some couples have decided to adopt, given the legal uncertainties. In some cases, couples who live in the quasi-marriage jurisdictions, where they can only register as domestic partners or enter into a civil union, they may do so and still travel to a recognition state to become married. The federal government has made clear that virtually all of the federal benefits that stem from marriage stem from marriage alone, and not other forms of recognition, such as civil union or domestic partnership. So, maybe the "belt and suspenders" approach, for now, makes most sense.

Take, for example the couples who went to Vermont, in the early 1990s to become civil union partners. For a while, that legal status only had an effect in Vermont, and was more symbolic for those who traveled there but returned home to another state having been "civilly joined". In October 2008, the *Wall Street Journal* reported on a couple, Daniel McNeil and Patrick Canavan who had been married four times—to each other![3] The couple first had a church wedding in D.C. in 1998, with no legal effect, then secured a civil union in Vermont, later became registered domestic partners in D.C., and finally were lawfully married in California. With each step, they gained certain (limited) legal rights as a couple.

But what about the couples who get married in a recognition state, and return home to a non-recognition state? Are they still married? What if we simply go on vacation, or a business trip, to the non-recognition state: Do we become unmarried when we cross state lines? And then, is the marriage revived at the border on the return trip? Well, the short answer to this question is we still don't know. Different states will take a different approach to this question, and in each case, it will depend on how and why it is being asked. Again, the law in this area is not entirely new since for years states have had different marriage rules around issues relating to age, race and consanguinity (e.g., first cousins can marry in some states and not in others). The legal question about cross-border recognition is still being sorted out by the state courts. Unless or until the Supreme Court finds a constitutional right for all same-sex couples to be married, we will continue to have inconsistency in this area.

The biggest issues for many couples who seek to become married in a recognition state and return or move to a non-recognition state are:

1. What federal rights can they import into that non-recognition state and how?
2. What state law rights or benefits might they try to secure?
3. What happens if they need to get divorced?

Each of these questions is addressed below.

# Federal Rights:

As previously discussed, many federal benefits, like tax, employee benefits (including retirement) and immigration, have adopted the place of celebration rule, and therefore can indeed be imported into a state that otherwise does not recognize the marriage. For those federal rights that are based on place of domicile (like Social Security) then, returning to or moving to a non-recognition state forecloses those rights (unless, and until, the law changes).

There are essentially three categories of federal rights/benefits:

A. Rights stemming from place of celebration—meaning where lawful marriage was entered into, i.e., where the marriage license was validly issued and the marriage solemnized (not where the wedding "party" took place).

B. Rights stemming from place of domicile—meaning the federal government will look to the state law of where the couple resides at the time of application for benefits to determine whether they are "married" and eligible.

C. Rights stemming from being married, or some other quasi-marriage status, such as civil union or domestic partnership—it is unclear yet whether the federal government agency administering the program will look to place of celebration vs. place of domicile, or recognize the quasi-marriage status for the benefit. This is the "unclear" bucket. It will change periodically as new regulations or guidance are issued from the agencies, or as the courts address the discrepancies.

## A. Place of Celebration:

Several benefits are now available to same-sex couples married in a state that recognizes their union, regardless of where they currently reside. These include:

1. Federal Taxes

   As mentioned, the IRS recently issued Revenue Ruling 2013-17, which declares that federal rights and benefits for tax matters are available to same-sex married couples according to their place of celebration. So, for the 2013 tax year, all legally married same-sex couples will be required to file their returns together as either "married filing jointly" or "married filing separately," no matter where the couple currently resides. In addition, already married couples can go back and amend their returns (if favorable for them to receive a refund) for the "open" years, which is usually the past three.

2. Employee Benefits (Including Retirement Plans)

   Also already covered is the DOL ruling about all employee benefits that are governed by federal law, such as pension and retirement plans. These will now be available to all lawfully married same-sex couples irrespective of where they live. It will be important for all married couples (or upon marriage) to change/update their beneficiary designation forms for all retirement plan benefits. If you are already in "pay-out" status and did not elect a spousal survivor option, you should contact your plan administrator to request a retroactive change.

3. Immigration

   Where the marriage took place currently determines whether a foreign spouse can immediately apply for U.S. citizenship, according to the U.S. Citizenship and Immigration Services (USCIS). Specifically, the USCIS website states, "As a general matter, the law of the place where the marriage was celebrated determines whether the marriage is legally valid for immigration purposes."[4] That means that U.S. citizens can file immigrant visa petitions on behalf of their same-sex spouses immediately.

4. Military and Veteran Benefits

Military and veterans benefits now flow to spouses of same-sex spouses based on whether their marriage occurred in a state that legally recognizes the relationship.

5. Federal Employee Benefits

All federal employees who are in a same-sex marriage are eligible for all spousal benefits, such as healthcare, disability and retirement effective immediately. If you did not change your plan elections during the open window in the summer of 2013, you will need to do so at the next open enrollment period, as announced by the Office of Personnel Management.

6. Federal Ethics Rules

There are a host of ethics rules for both federal employees and elected officials that also extend to spouses, including the prohibition of taking gifts above certain limits. This is to avoid the issue or appearance of bribing a governmental official. On August 19, 2013, the Office of Government Ethics issued an opinion stating that these rules have now all been extended to all same-sex married spouses, based on being validly married somewhere, but specifically exclude couples in either civil unions or domestic partnerships.[5]

7. Federal Elections Commission Rules

Similarly, federal election laws provide certain campaign contribution limits for married couples and have also decided, in light of the *Windsor* decision, that these rules should apply to all lawfully married same-sex couples, irrespective of where they reside, and therefore based on the place of celebration rule.[6]

## B. Place of Domicile:

Some benefits, however, still are only available to same-sex married couples based on where they live, rather than where their marriage actually took place. This is referred to as the place of domicile rule, which looks to whether the state in which you reside for legal purposes recognizes your marriage. The effect of these rules is that some same-sex couples lawfully married in a recognition state may no longer have these rights if they return or move to a non-recognition state. These include:

1. Social Security

   The Social Security Administration is required under statute to limit payment of claims to same-sex couples who would otherwise be able to inherit (without a will) under that state's intestacy laws.[7] This has the effect for now of applying the place of domicile rule for these benefits. Couples who were married in a recognition state, and then return home to a state that does not recognize their marriage, do not currently qualify for spousal Social Security benefits. (Interestingly, couples who hold a civil union or domestic partner registration of the "flavor" that provides inheritance rights should be eligible for these same benefits based on this statute.)

2. Medicaid

   Some states may provide hardship protection for partners of a person in long-term care, but eligibility for other Medicaid protections is dependent on the state's recognition of the marriage.[8]

3. Family Medical Leave Act ("FMLA") for Non-Federal Employees

   FMLA provides up to twelve weeks of unpaid leave in any 12-month period to a spouse of someone with a serious health condition. Place of domicile is used to determine eligibility based on guidance issued by the Department of Labor in August 2013.[9] It would appear that employers in non-recognition states are not required, but may voluntarily choose, to extend Family Medical Leave to same-sex married spouses.

4. Temporary Assistance for Needy Families

Temporary Assistance for Needy Families (TANF) is a federally-funded program administered sometimes slightly differently by each state. Essentially, it provides certain assistance to low-income parents and their children. States may have different names for their version of this program, such as public assistance, temporary assistance, general assistance or cash assistance.

TANF includes a requirement that adult recipients work or participate in a welfare-to-work program, although the requirements vary from state to state. In many states, being eligible for TANF may also make you eligible for free child care.

This program, for now, is available only for same-sex married couples (or single parents formerly of a same-sex couple) in recognition states.

For more information on eligibility and restrictions, see:

www.hrc.org/files/assets/resources/Post-DOMA_TANF_v3.pdf

5. Copyright Laws

Federal copyright laws extend certain rights based on marriage. For now, these seem to be governed by the marriage being recognized where the couple is domiciled.[10]

## C. "We Don't Know Yet" Category of Federal Benefits

There are still some benefits that may or may not be available, based on place of celebration or place of domicile, because the relevant agency that administers these laws has not yet issued regulations stating what affect the *Windsor* decision has on them. An example of this are the Securities and Exchange Act laws relating to disclosure requirements of publically held securities by spouses. See Appendix B for a list of web resources for updates on these regulations.

What has become clear is that the quasi-marriage status of domestic partnership and civil unions is not marriage for federal law purposes. Although many states attempted to provide "all" of the same rights and privileges as marriage in their statutes (like New Jersey, for example), the federal government seems to be making clear in its regulations interpreting and implementing the *Windsor* case that federal benefits related to marriage do not extend to civil unions or domestic partnerships. (See IRS Ruling 2013-17.)

**What This Means**

Although these categories and rules seem clear, many federal rights and benefits are administered by state agencies. For those non-recognition states being asked to implement these new federal rules, it may be a challenge and is bound to create chaos and uncertainty. Just take a look at the Texas National Guard, for example. The federal government has directed all branches of the military to process requests from same-sex married couples for benefits, and yet Texas and Mississippi are resistant.

The Texas Military Forces Commanding General went so far as to state, "because the Texas Constitution defines marriage as between a man and a woman, his state agency couldn't process applications from gay and lesbian couples."[11] He then provided information on nearby federal installations where the Guardsman could go to apply for benefits. Some spouses are being directed to military posts in other areas to get the ID card necessary to qualify for benefits, in defiance of national law. How long such nonsense will last is anyone's guess, but it is important to be aware of the issue.

## State Rights

Virtually all of the state rights that flow from marriage are likely not available in non-recognition states unless they become one of the hybrid non-recognition states that chooses to recognize out-of-state same-sex marriages, like Oregon recently did. (For a complete list of those states as of this writing, see Table A.1 in Appendix A.) However, this area is the most fluid and seems to be changing almost daily.

Take, for example, the couple from Ohio that was mentioned in the preface. John Arthur and James Obergefell, who reside in (and returned to)

Ohio, were married in Maryland. Yet, the federal judge in that case said that the state official was required to issue a (state) death certificate listing them as "married" for purposes of those (state) official records. Presumably, that will affect benefit claims that the survivor may make, and perhaps only those benefits that are governed by federal law will be required, but not the state ones. The truth is, we really don't know.

Similarly, in Pennsylvania, when Sarah Ellyn Farley passed away, the federal judge ordered her employer to issue the survivor annuity payment on her deferred compensation plan to her spouse, not her parents, even though Pennsylvania does not recognize the marriage.[12] Presumably the employer's benefit plan in question is governed by Pennsylvania state law, but, it is regulated by federal legislation as a qualified plan under ERISA.

These are only two examples of hundreds, or even thousands, that will start to occur every day. People will make claims in part to see, in some instances, how their local authorities react. Where the answer is not favorable, more court cases will undoubtedly be pursued (for those who can afford to take such measures) and more clarity will result.

### Divorce

Divorce is never a happy topic. Although there is precious little data available on the divorce rate of same-sex couples, it is probably fair to assume that we will be no better off than our straight counter-parts in this regard. It is possible, therefore, that roughly half of same-sex couples who get married may wind up also getting divorced—or at least have the desire to do so. The tricky part is in the actual application of how divorce laws work.

Like marriage, they differ on a state-by-state basis, and, as the Supreme Court reminded us in *Windsor*, it is an area of the law exclusively regulated by the states. Most states do not take jurisdiction over a marriage unless the parties are resident or domiciled in its state. Some states have begun to allow non-resident same-sex couples to seek a divorce there, since they recognize that many non-recognition states, won't recognize same-sex marriage for purposes of allowing its state's family courts to dissolve it in a divorce proceeding.

Several states have made exceptions for non-resident same-sex couples to come to them to get divorced. This is usually provided that divorce is not available to them where they live, and some states require that couples were married there to start with—even if they are no longer residents at the time they are seeking divorce. The states where this is possible currently include California, Minnesota, Delaware, the District of Columbia, Wyoming and Vermont. The conditions for divorce to be available for out-of-state same-sex couples in each of these states can vary.

In the case of Vermont, for example, they allow non-resident same-sex couples to divorce there only if there are no minor children involved (and therefore no custody issues). And the couple must come from a state that does not otherwise permit or allow same-sex divorce. Otherwise, they won't hear the case.

Interestingly, Wyoming is the only non-recognition state that allows same-sex divorce. So, ironically, they won't allow you to get married there, but they will happily help you terminate your same-sex marriage, even if you don't live there, provided your home state doesn't allow it.[13] The rules in this area stem either from case law or statute. For example, two women, residents of Wyoming, were married in Canada and attempted to divorce in Wyoming. The Supreme Court of Wyoming allowed the divorce, saying that the recognition of residents' same-sex marriage from another jurisdiction for the specific purpose of a divorce proceeding was not the same as recognition of same-sex marriage. Whereas, in the District of Columbia, a bill was passed in 2012 that said that same-sex couples married in Washington, D.C., do not have to be residents for the District to grant them a divorce.[14]

So, even though many couples from the thirty-five non-recognition states can, and increasingly are, shuttling off to Provincetown or San Francisco (or other recognition locations) to get married and return to their home (non-recognition) states, they may face a rude awakening if they need to get divorced. Some states, for instance, will only take jurisdiction over the marriage if the couple is a resident of that state, as evidenced by filing a state income tax return (among other things). This then, becomes the "double whammy" for couples, say, from Florida, where there is no state income tax. If, for example, they need to move back to Massachusetts or

New York to get divorced, not only do they have to experience the pain and costs associated with that, but they may also be subject to a state income tax where they had not previously been. Not to mention the fact that moving is disruptive and expensive. Very few couples go into marriage thinking about divorce, but it is something everyone needs to consider, particularly same-sex couples who may live or move to a non-recognition state.

Unfortunately, the answer for many unhappy same-sex couples today, at least in the non-recognition states, is to stay put, separate and try to sort out their issues in some other way. The problem with this resolution, now that the IRS has adopted the place of celebration rule, is that, separated or not, the IRS will continue to regard the couple as married, for all federal tax filing purposes, unless, or until, they actually get divorced. This presents a real dilemma for many. The other problem with this solution gets compounded by couples who couldn't get divorced, but who have happily proceeded to get remarried. While that may work for them personally, the law is unlikely to recognize the subsequent marriage, and will still consider the first marriage to be in place for federal tax purposes.

## How Does Divorce Differ for Those Living in or Moving to a Non-Recognition State?

When gay marriage first became lawful in Massachusetts, then-Governor Romney feared, among other things, that Massachusetts would soon become the "Las Vegas for gay weddings,"[15] thinking that same-sex couples from all over the U.S. would travel to Massachusetts to become married and then return home and claim certain rights or benefits. Indeed, heterosexual couples have for some time come home to where they were raised to be married in their parents' church or synagogue, and then returned home in a different state to find themselves still married.

It has long since been the case, under the "full faith and credit" clause of the U.S. Constitution that states will give full recognition to laws of other states. But this is not the case with same-sex marriage. There has been some debate and litigation on this subject over the years, and I predict that this will only increase, due to inconsistencies in the law between recognition and non-recognition states.

In Massachusetts, Governor Romney's fear never materialized. Yes, some couples did come to Massachusetts in the euphoria of the historic *Goodridge* decision to become married. But, the Governor dusted off an old law from 1913 that required applicants for a marriage license in Massachusetts to be residents here. This put these carpet-baggers to a screeching halt while he was still in office.* Fortunately, common sense prevailed and the legislature of the Commonwealth overturned the antiquated 1913 law, thus allowing non-residents to marry in Massachusetts. However, the predicted onslaught didn't happen. The reason for this was twofold: 1) When the couple returned to their non-recognition state, their marriage was not recognized for state law purposes; and 2) Under DOMA, the marriage also wasn't recognized for federal purposes. So those marriages were perhaps more symbolic than legal.

Over time, however, some states (like New York and Maryland) began, through lower court decisions in each state, to recognize same-sex marriages that were validly performed and entered into in another jurisdiction.[16] There are many cases pending in states around the country on this issue of recognizing out-of-state marriages, even if they could not be performed in the home state.

*When You Move*

So what happens when you move? How about when you just visit another state? Am I still married when my husband and I take our nieces and nephew to Disney World in Florida? If I need to go to the hospital for emergency surgery while I'm there, can he see me in the hospital? Can he make medical decisions in Florida for me if I'm unconscious?

What happens if gay parents who conceived in a recognition state, using assisted reproductive technology, move to a non-recognition state? Are they both protected as parents without a second parent adoption? What if

---

* Massachusetts General Laws Chapter 207, Section 11, known as the "1913 Law" was enacted during a period of legal uncertainty surrounding interracial marriage. On July 15, 2008, the Massachusetts State Senate unanimously voted to repeal the 1913 law, and then on July 29, the House also voted 118 to 35 to repeal it. Governor Patrick signed the bill into law on July 31, 2008, and it took effect immediately.

they do not have a joint-custody agreement, or they have such an agreement, but it was not approved by a court?

These issues are more fully addressed in Chapters 7 and 8. But it is important to be aware of them, and to know that they are still being debated. In some instances, these are questions that are being presented, almost daily, to judges in federal and state courts around the country.

Imagine, for a moment, that your straight friends who now live in Chicago return home to their family in New York to be married. Is there any question that after being married in New York the couple may not be considered still married in Chicago? While the straight couple may not have any question, a same-sex couple in the same situation does today.

There are a variety of reasons for this. To start with, many states still have "mini-DOMAs" on the books and have not yet (under the conflict-of-law principles) afforded recognition to out-of-state gay marriages. In addition, under Section 2 of DOMA, which is still valid, the impediment still exists for same-sex married couples, since Section 2 states:

> "[N]o State, territory, or possession of the United States, or Indian tribe, shall be required to give effect to any public act, record, or judicial proceeding of any other State, territory, possession, or tribe respecting a relationship between persons of the same-sex that is treated as a marriage under the laws of such other State, territory, possession, or tribe, or a right or claim arising from such relationship."

It remains to be seen whether these laws will indeed meet constitutional muster under either the federal constitutional laws governing equal protection or due process, or both. This is discussed more fully in the final chapter of this book.

Fortunately, many years ago, our founding fathers contemplated this type of problem when they drafted the United States Constitution. Since we have a federal system, they reserved for the federal government the power to make laws in certain areas, and all the rest were left to the states. These include, as we now know, all laws governing family relations, including marriage and adoption. Since there was a chance that each state might react differently on a variety of points, they also added a provision to the Constitution called the "Full Faith and Credit" clause, which states:

> *"Full faith and credit shall be given in each state to the public acts, records, and judicial proceedings of every other state. And the Congress may by general laws prescribe the manner in which such acts, records, and proceedings shall be proved, and the effect thereof."*

Whether Section 2 of DOMA violates this, or other laws that still exist in many states, remains to be seen. In August 2007, a federal appeals court held that the clause did require Oklahoma to issue a revised birth certificate showing both adoptive parents of a child born in Oklahoma who had been adopted by a same-sex couple married in another state.[17] Another federal appeals court held differently in April 2011 in a Louisiana case, *Adar v. Smith.*[18] Eventually, it is possible the Supreme Court may need to resolve this issue. However, the constitutional arguments around the full faith and credit clause are not likely the stronger ones when it comes to getting uniform recognition of same-sex marriages.

The Supreme Court, however, long ago carved out a public policy exception for this constitutional provision that has the effect of narrowing its scope to apply only to judgments and not to laws of other states, where the conflicting law is based on important public policy reasons from another state.*

The real action, until the Supreme Court weighs in again on the big issue of whether same-sex couples have a constitutional right to be married, will happen in the state courts under the conflict of laws arguments.

---

* In 1939, the Court in *Pacific Employers Insurance v. Industrial Accident* wrote:

"There are some limitations upon the extent to which a state may be required by the full faith and credit clause to enforce even the judgment of another state in contravention of its own statutes or policy. See *Wisconsin v. Pelican Insurance Co.*, 127 U.S. 265; *Huntington v. Attrill*, 146 U.S. 657; *Finney v. Guy*, 189 U.S. 335; see also *Clarke v. Clarke*, 178 U.S. 186; *Olmsted v. Olmsted*, 216 U.S. 386; *Hood v. McGehee*, 237 U.S. 611; cf. *Gasquet v. Fenner*, 247 U.S. 16. In the case of statutes, the full faith and credit clause does not require one state to substitute for its own statute, applicable to persons and events within it, the conflicting statute of another state, even though that statute is of controlling force in the courts of the state of its enactment with respect to the same persons and events."

They go something like this: Generally, states have always applied a "place of celebration" rule to recognition of marriages. That is to say, if the marriage was valid where solemnized, then it would be valid in the state. The reason for this rule is to provide stability and avoid these very problems that could arise if marriage status changed state by state. Indeed, this has been codified in the "Uniform Marriage and Divorce Act" of 1970, subsequently adopted by twenty-three states. The general exception to this rule is when the marriage from another state would violate a "strong public policy" of the state. Examples of this that have been accepted by courts in the past have to do with polygamous or incestuous marriages. These rules are more clear when the state has a law on the books that specifically calls out the offensive aspects as opposed to simply not preferring it for their own residents. This was often the case with inter-racial marriage.

In fact, in one of the earliest reported decisions on this point, a judge in Massachusetts in 1873 articulated the rule this way:

> *"A marriage which is prohibited here by statute, because contrary to the policy of our laws, is yet valid if celebrated elsewhere according to the laws of the place, even if the parties are citizens and residents of this Commonwealth, and have gone abroad for the purpose of evading our laws, unless the Legislature has clearly enacted that such marriages out of the stae shall have no validity here."[19]*

The anti-gay marriage laws in most states today simply define marriage for their state law purposes (of issuing a marriage license) as between one man and on woman. Some of the laws go on to say that same-sex marriages are "void" or "prohibited" in their state, but rarely address the public policy issue of whether out-of-state marriages should also not be respected.*

---

* The Virginia statute is, however, one that goes so far as to say that, "Any marriages entered into by persons of the same sex in another state or jurisdiction shall be void in all respects in Virginia and any contractual rights created by such marriage shall be void and unenforceable." Va. Code Ann. Sect. 20-45.2. Given the extreme position taken by this state's legislature, it is possible that this statute may be more vulnerable to be overturned as unconstitutional.

There is a long line of case law, following that decision in 1873 where courts in states recognized out-of-state marriages therefore, even when the marriage would not have been allowed or was "offensive" to the home state.[20] It is expected that this jurisprudence will be relied upon again by same-sex couples who marry in a recognition state and return home to a non-recognition state.

Until this gets resolved, it is precisely why, when gay and lesbian couples become married in a recognition state and move to, or even travel to, a non-recognition state, they should still have some additional legal protections in place, such as powers of attorney, healthcare proxies and living wills to protect them in case the awful thing happens. All of these items are discussed in more detail in Chapter 8.

But, right now, there is precious little a couple can do to ensure that their legal rights and benefits of marriage will travel with them. For that, we will need to await further guidance from our court system, including, likely another case by the United States Supreme Court to settle the issue. So stay tuned.

## Proxy Marriages

What if you're in a non-recognition state and want to get married, but can't travel? Interestingly, some states (and foreign countries) permit something called a "proxy marriage." This is where someone stands in for you (sort of like a power of attorney) and gets married on your behalf. While this may sound like a crazy idea, its genesis makes sense. It started out for military personnel who were deployed overseas and couldn't, precisely because of their deployment, get home to "tie-the-knot." Some states only allow proxy marriage for active duty military personnel.[21] For those that allow it, some states, such as Colorado, allow only one party to have a "proxy." Others, such as Montana, allow "double proxy" weddings. Neither of those states are recognition states yet, so it is yet to be seen whether this may ever be useful for a same-sex couple.

But what about Brazil? Interestingly, Brazil now allows both double proxy marriage and same-sex marriage and does not have a residency requirement.[22] The home state in the U.S., therefore, may or may not recognize the marriage, depending on whether it is a recognition state, but the federal government likely would recognize the marriage, so long as it was valid under the laws where it was performed. Think of the possibilities! Maybe some day each person would just dial into a justice of the peace in a friendly jurisdiction—on Skype, for instance—and get married. Undoubtedly, as the patchwork of laws continues, so, too, will forum shopping for states and countries with friendly laws that permit couples to obtain these very important rights.

# CHAPTER 7

# Family Planning and Children's Issues in Considering Marriage

The overwhelming majority of public policy areas in the U.S. are affected by the structure of U.S. government. Family law is one of those. The fact that the Constitution created two levels of government—federal and state—and gave each level particular powers dramatically affects who makes policy in a particular area. This system is known as "federalism."

Federalism can be a "blessing" or a "burden" for political activists who work toward policy change. The "blessing" comes from the practicality of being able to incrementally make changes state by state in a policy area, as opposed to having to be all or nothing at the federal level. The "burden," of course, is that this takes more time, effort and money. Our founding fathers (and mothers) specifically reserved family law issues to the states and the *Windsor* case confirmed this again.

An example of the blessing and burden of incremental change in the area of family law is in the *Goodridge* case. The Massachusetts' Supreme Judicial Court ruled that denying same-sex couples the right to marry was a violation of equal protection under the Massachusetts Constitution. So in the face of considerable federal governmental opposition to same-sex marriage, and regardless of the issue assuming a major emphasis in presidential and congressional campaigns, the Massachusetts Court had jurisdiction to decide who could wed, since there was no U.S. Supreme Court ruling to the contrary.

This is similar to the way in which states decide who will get a driver's license, or at what age a person may have an alcoholic drink. This last example may surprise some people, since the legal drinking age in every state is twenty-one. But this standard did not come from federal legislation. Rather, each state at its own pace enacted legislation to this effect. It should be noted, however, that there was considerable pressure from the Reagan Administration that federal highway funds would be withheld from states that didn't enact such legislation. So as you can see, the federal government often uses financial coercion to achieve state compliance on certain issues.

## So What about Family Law?

In the aftermath of the U. S. Supreme Court's *Windsor* decision, many aspects of family law may have to be reviewed, especially in those states that recognize same-sex marriage. It is very likely that *Windsor* will give birth (pun intended) to a flurry of litigation. Indeed, it already has. With that said, many of the topics covered here are not new to same-sex couples who create families. It is likely that these issues, particularly as they relate to children, may simply get more or different attention now in light of *Windsor* because families of same-sex couples are more commonly understood as part of the broader community.

This chapter does not purport to be an extensive analysis of existing family law, either as it relates to heterosexual families or same-sex families. The literature in both of these areas is vast.[1] An excellent work on same-sex family law, and one of my favorite resource tools as a lawyer, is the very comprehensive volume by Courtney G. Joslin and Shannon P. Minter, *Lesbian, Gay, Bisexual and Transgender Family Law*, 12th ed. (West Publishing). My aim here is to provide an overview of some of the likely issues same-sex families face, and how these may change in the recognition states.

Just a few of the areas of same-sex family law that are likely to draw attention following *Windsor* are:

- Adoption law

- Custody determinations in the event that a same-sex marriage is dissolved

- Assisted reproduction therapies (ART)

- Separated parents where divorce is not possible

- Transsexual parents

- Children's rights in the case of transgender children, especially parental views

## Children of Same-Sex Marriages/Families

Regardless of parental sexual orientation, children enjoy or suffer the confines of the situation into which they are born or adopted. Controversy surrounding same-sex parenting has abounded, and is discussed below.

At this juncture, though, it is worth taking a look at some very wise words uttered almost sixty years ago in a landmark Supreme Court ruling. *Brown v. Board of Education* is enlightening on the subject of what effects policies have on children.

NAACP Chief Counsel Thurgood Marshall argued that segregation has a psychological effect on both black and white children, despite some concerns among his colleagues that using social science data might not hold sway with the justices. Marshall cited "doll studies" that had been conducted by psychologist Kenneth Clark in which Clark observed that there was a negative psychological impact on children of both races who played only with white dolls.[2] Black children developed an inferiority complex, while white children felt superior. Of course, the entire social milieu of the country at the time set the scene for these differing senses of self. But this social science data ended up being included in the chief justice's writing of the 9-0 Supreme Court decision.

I do not believe it inappropriate to apply the observations of the effects on children's psyche to the children of same-sex parents. Although the social and political climates in the U. S. are moving with extraordinary momentum toward the view that everyone has a right to love and to marry, it is quite likely that children of same-sex parents face questions from their peers and perhaps even bullying. The bold statement made in *Windsor* acknowledging that the plaintiff's marriage had to be recognized by the federal government is a victory toward affirming the family of the child in a same-sex marriage/relationship.

But marriage carries with it advantages and disadvantages, which same-sex couples should carefully consider before taking action, especially when children are involved. In addition to the benefits of marriage already mentioned, there are additional benefits that flow to couples with children that you should be aware of if you are considering becoming parents. Despite lingering cultural bias against same-sex couples creating and raising families, children of same-sex parents have been found to grow and thrive in ways that mirror children of heterosexual couples. "One comprehensive study of children raised by lesbian mothers or gay fathers concluded that children raised by same-sex parents did not differ from other children in terms of emotional functioning, sexual orientation, stigmatization, gender role behavior, behavioral adjustment, gender identity, learning and grade point averages. Where research differences have been found, they have sometimes favored same-sex parents."[3]

What is clear is that along with an increased number of same-sex marriages, generally, so, too, are these couples having children and creating family. According to the 2000 U.S. Census, "33 percent of female same-sex couple households and 22 percent of male same-sex couple households reported at least one child under eighteen living in their home."[4]

In a report from The Future of Children, a collaboration between Princeton University and the Brookings Institute, William Meezan and Jonathan Rauch observe that marriage for same-sex couples confers three types of benefits to children being raised by such couples: 1) Material well-being through benefits such as financial stability, health insurance, and family leave, 2) Increased durability and stability of their parents' relationship, and 3) Increased social acceptance of and support for same-sex families.[5]

# Material Well-Being

Married couples with children enjoy a number of added financial benefits that single parents do not. These include:

## Increased Tax Deductions

Married couples—same-sex or heterosexual—have the option to file tax returns jointly, thereby doubling their standard deduction to $11,900 (from $5,950 for single taxpayers), and if they have children, they can take $3,800 per child as a dependent exemption.* Unmarried couples must file separately, and only one parent can claim a child as a dependent. (It may be advantageous, however, for a single person to file as "head of household"— so marriage, here, may not be a pure income tax benefit when children are involved.) As with all income tax issues, please consult a competent CPA for advice about what is best for your situation.

## Child Tax Credit

In addition, if you and your spouse make less than $110,000 a year, you are also entitled to the Child Tax Credit of $1,000 per child, which is phased out as your household income rises above the $110,000 maximum. Lower income families may receive a credit of more than $1,000 per child. However, again, marriage may not always put you in a better position here for this benefit. A single person can earn up to $75,000 and qualify for this credit and, in this instance, the unmarried partner has no limit on what he or she may earn, assuming that the partner is not also a legal parent. What is important to remember here, as well, is that this federal benefit is only available to taxpayers who are related to the child biologically or by adoption. Here, marriage may not suffice. Same-sex partners who are raising children in states that don't permit second parent adoptions may be at a disadvantage.

---

* All dollar amounts listed in this section are from the Internal Revenue Code and regulations in effect in 2013. They are subject to change in later years.

## Family and Medical Leave Act

Same-sex married couples who live in a recognition state are now entitled to the benefits available through the Family and Medical Leave Act (FMLA). According to the Department of Labor, FMLA applies to all public agencies, all public and private elementary and secondary schools, and companies with fifty or more employees. These employers must provide an eligible employee with up to twelve weeks of unpaid leave each year for any of the following reasons:

- For the birth and care of the newborn child of an employee;
- For placement with the employee of a child for adoption or foster care;
- To care for an immediate family member (spouse, child, or parent) with a serious health condition; or
- To take medical leave when the employee is unable to work because of a serious health condition.[6]

Qualifying for the FMLA now allows same-sex married couples who work for organizations with more than fifty employees assurance that they will be able to care for their children, or each other, for up to three months, should one of them become injured or ill. This is without the risk of losing their job, as there is now a guarantee that their job must be there when they return.

## Family Health Insurance Deduction

Per the IRS, same-sex married couples who file jointly can also now enjoy the deduction of employer-paid health insurance that heterosexual couples have long taken advantage of. Some estimate the value of that change to be worth more than $1,000 per couple per year. For companies where employee health insurance coverage is only available to spouses and families, it should now be more readily available.

## *Social Security Benefits to Surviving Children*

Social Security benefits are not as clear-cut, however, since the Social Security Administration is currently required by statute to apply the place of domicile rule. It, therefore, only recognizes a marriage if your state of residence recognizes it at the time you apply for benefits. This may change, since we are still waiting for further guidance from the SSA. However, if otherwise eligible, the benefits can be considerable for children of parents who die or become disabled. Essentially, children are entitled to Social Security benefits if they are the biological or adoptive child of a parent who dies or becomes disabled. There is some question about whether they may also be available to children born into a same-sex marriage if the family lives in a state where second parent adoption is not available.

# Durability of the Relationship

Although data on same-sex marriages and divorces is slim, 2010 Census data currently indicates that same-sex couples have fewer divorces than their opposite-sex couple counterparts. Part of the reason for the disparity may be that same-sex couples who finally now have the opportunity to legally marry have been together for many years and were less likely to split because of their enduring bond. Stated another way, those married recently have sustained and worked through issues by virtue of having been in committed relationships for some time, and were previously unmarried because marriage was not legally available to them. The other reason may be that the data is scarce and too new. Or, the data could simply be wrong or misleading, since so many states don't allow same-sex couples to become divorced. Whatever the reason, it is possible that same-sex couples who take the step to marry mean to really be committed to one another and stay married. An author and scholar from the Brookings Institute, Jonathan Rauch, has suggested in his work that same-sex couples who do take the step of marrying are generally more stable than same-sex couples who do not. And the impact on the children of the relationship is less disruptive. Stability is good for kids.

In addition to reducing the chances that a relationship will dissolve, marriage also provides children with formal proof that their parents are committed to one another and to their family. Such a commitment, and the stability it provides, can be comforting and beneficial to a child.

## Increased Social Acceptance of Same-Sex Relationships

For the last decade, acceptance of same-sex relationships, in general, and same-sex marriages, in particular, has risen sharply. A Gallup poll reported that public support for legalizing gay marriage has risen from 42 percent in 2004 to more than 50 percent in 2011.[7] Such public support for same-sex marriage can only benefit children, whose self-image is, in part, defined by their parents. Knowing that their parents' relationship has been recognized and approved by the government, and by extension, society in general, can only be beneficial for children.

In fact, Justice Anthony Kennedy's opinion on DOMA included commentary about the impact same-sex marriage can have on a child, and the damage caused when a union is not recognized. He said, "It humiliates tens of thousands of children now being raised by same-sex couples . . . The law in question makes it even more difficult for the children to understand the integrity and closeness of their own family and its concord with other families in their community and in their daily lives."[8]

That said, having married parents, regardless of sexual orientation, is good for children because society generally approves of married families more than unmarried families. Parents who are not married are typically viewed as less committed to the relationship and the family—true or not—which impacts how outsiders view the family unit.

## Sperm Donation

Lesbian couples interested in starting or expanding a family frequently rely on sperm donation to effect a pregnancy. However, the source of the sperm is an important decision to be made, with potentially serious legal consequences. Sperm donors can be known, as from a friend or acquaintance, or unknown, typically chosen through a sperm bank.

## Known Sperm Donor

Although some women opt to use sperm donated by someone they know, perhaps for simplicity, or because they admire the person, this can create unexpected and unwanted legal issues. The first step in this case is to ensure the sperm donor's parental rights are completely terminated from the start. Work with an attorney to ensure this occurs and make sure they really know the law in this area. Usually, a simple written agreement where the donor relinquishes all rights and the mother absolves him from all obligations is helpful, but insufficient, since these agreements are not enforceable in court. Child support, generally, is for the benefit of the child, not the parents. As a general matter, in addition to such an agreement, there needs to be a formal (judicially approved) adoption that recognizes (and extinguishes) parental rights.

Donor agreements are also an option, whereby the sperm donor may agree to avoid certain high-risk sexual behavior until the donation has been made, may agree to give up his parental rights, or abide by restrictions from contacting the minor child set by the mothers, as well as to address what should happen to any sperm that is leftover following the procedure. An LGBT-savvy attorney can draft such an agreement to ensure that your intentions, and those of your donor, are fully expressed and carried out.

## Unknown Sperm Donor

To avoid any question of paternal parentage, many couples work with a sperm bank and use anonymously-donated sperm.

However, depending on the medical procedure used, one or both women can be biological parents of the child. Using reciprocal IVF, donated sperm and an egg donated by one of the women, which is then fertilized and placed in the other woman's uterus, both women can be biological parents. This is a fairly recent development in the world of alternative reproductive therapies (ART), since for many years courts held that a child could only have one mother.[9] However, recently, courts have recognized that two woman can both be legal mothers of a child.[10]

## Surrogacy

Gay couples who want to become parents and lesbian couples who are having difficulty conceiving are increasingly turning to gestational surrogates to carry their babies. Using a known or anonymous egg donor, gay couples can establish a biological tie to the baby so that at least one father can establish parental rights from the outset. Lesbians can choose to use one of their eggs, or also go the donated egg route, along with donated sperm. While success with gestational surrogacy and techniques in alternative reproductive technology are improving, the cost to have a baby via gestational surrogacy can range from $130,000 to $170,000 in major U.S. cities.[11] Smaller cities, like Portland, Oregon, are becoming especially popular because of the lower costs of conception and delivery, and the higher rates of success. Portland's Oregon Reproductive Medicine claims an 85 percent surrogacy success rate, which is much higher than average.[12] And many international couples often head to the U.S. because their countries do not allow surrogacy.

In the U.S., surrogacy is illegal in eleven states and the District of Columbia. Some of these states even criminalize such arrangements, while six states have approved surrogacy contracts.[13] It is important to work with an experienced attorney before beginning the surrogacy process. The agreements donors sign may include language that does not reflect the couple's intent. Check your state's current position on it to avoid unexpected and unwanted consequences. As states are changing their regulations regarding same-sex marriage, so, too, are they expected to change their regulations regarding surrogacy.

# Adoption

Adoption is on the rise among same-sex couples. According to data from demographer Gary Gates of the University of California, Los Angeles, "nineteen percent of same-sex couples who were raising children in 2009 reported an adopted child as a member of the household, up from eight percent in 2000. Gates estimates that four percent of the adopted population in the United States—about 65,000 children—live in homes in which the head of the household is gay or lesbian."[14] Unfortunately, there are still many states that prohibit same-sex couples from adopting.*

## Adoption of Non-Biological Children

In states where same-sex marriage is recognized, adoption is typically—but not always—an easier process. When a married couple adopts in a recognition state, both parties are the adoptive parents from the outset. However, in states where same-sex marriage is not recognized, adoption becomes trickier, and not at all uniform. In those states, single-parent adoption by a person who is gay or lesbian may be available, but their partner is not always able to adopt as well. The child may live in a two-parent household, but only have one legal parent.

Sadly, there are also states that have policies that effectively restrict same-sex couples from adopting or fostering children, giving preference to opposite-sex married couples and singles. These include, but are not limited to, Ohio, Utah, and Mississippi.[15] Thankfully, there are other states, namely California, Maryland, Massachusetts, Nevada, New Jersey, and New York, that expressly prohibit discrimination on the basis of sexual orientation in adoptions and foster placements.[16]

Married couples with children who live in recognition states should pursue second-parent adoption, also known as co-parent adoption, immediately. With a formal adoption, both partners are legal parents and guardians. This is a critical point. That step reduces any chance of a child being placed in foster care following the death of either parent, whether in a recognition state or not. It is a necessity for same-sex married couples to protect their children.

---

* Florida, Mississippi, and Utah explicitly prohibit same-sex couples and individuals from adopting children. Michigan prohibits same-sex couples from adopting by statutory construction, but not LGBT individuals. Source: Liberty Counsel, Same-Sex Adoption Laws by State. http://www.lc.org/profamily/samesex_adoption_by_state.pdf

### *Adoption of One Spouse's Biological Child*

Adoption can also be important when marriages end and the couple separates. In situations where one spouse is the birth parent and the other would like to legally adopt their mutual child, the process is generally straightforward in recognition states. In non-recognition states, however, it is more difficult. Take the Fisher-Borne family of North Carolina, for example. Marcie and Chantelle Fisher-Borne have been together for sixteen years and were married in 2011 in Washington, D.C. But they live in North Carolina, which does not recognize their union. Even worse, North Carolina bans same-sex couples from second parent adoption. Since adoption law is governed by each state, the couple currently has no recourse.

That means that Marcie is their five-year-old daughter, Miley's, only legal parent, and Chantelle is their twenty-month-old son, Eli's, only legal parent.[17] Their fear surrounding what might happen if one of them dies led them to become the lead plaintiffs in an American Civil Liberties Union suit challenging the North Carolina adoption ban, and its ban on same-sex marriage. Filed in 2012, and amended in 2013, the lawsuit represents six same-sex couples who have been denied the right to marry and to adopt their partner's child(ren). The case is currently pending.

Adoption can also be important when marriages end and the couple separates.

## Custody Issues

While child custody can often be a sticking point for any couple that splits up, it can be considerably more complex for same-sex couples, married or not. That is because only one partner can possibly be the biological parent of the child or children. Some couples take the step of having the non-biological parent formally adopt the children to establish parental rights, but that doesn't always make custody issues easier if the couple later separates.

Consider the case out of York, Pennsylvania, involving a lesbian couple that registered a civil union in Vermont that was not recognized in Pennsylvania. One of the women was inseminated with a friend's sperm and bore two children. When the women ended their relationship, the birth mother took custody and relocated. The non-birth mother, who had never formally adopted the children, sued for physical and legal custody.[18]

The case went to the Pennsylvania Superior Court, and after a lengthy battle, the court gave custody to the two biological parents *and* the non-birth mother. The biological father and non-birth mother were also both ordered to pay child support to the birth mother, who had primary physical custody of the children. According to *The York Daily Record*, which reported on the case, "The court decided a child could have three parents."[19]

This is only one state's perspective (Pennsylvania's), however, and does not mean that your specific state will necessarily rule similarly. However, states including Delaware and Massachusetts, as well as the District of Columbia, now permit third-parent adoptions. Before pursuing adoption of any kind, however, it is important to know what your state permits.

# CHAPTER 8

# Life and Estate Planning, Whether Married or Not

In our law practice, we refer to the work we do as "life and estate planning." Often people contact us to help them put together their will. Usually what unfolds is the need for a legal plan—not only upon death—but during their lifetime to govern their assets and help identify important people to play a role in the unfortunate circumstances of catastrophic accidents or illness; dementia or old age issues; and eventually, to make decisions after one is gone. It is inevitable. Without a plan (and some legal documents supporting the plan), difficulties can arise, usually at the most inopportune times, either because of a serious health problem, or accident, or worse, because of a sudden death.

Whatever the occasion, it can be stressful for loved ones to deal with the necessities of life, like paying mortgages and other bills and helping to make medical decisions. In this chapter, I will review some of the basic life and estate planning elements that are necessary for all adults, and point out some particular issues for gay and lesbian couples when doing this work. To the extent that marriage factors into the life and estate planning discussion, I will point out that connection as well.

This is not meant to be the definitive work on estate planning for gay couples, however. That has already been done by, among others, my friend, Joan Burda: *Estate Planning for Gay Couples*.[1] While that book was written primarily by and for lawyers, it is a terrific comprehensive treatment of this entire subject matter. We also maintain a website for couples that contains updated and useful information: www.gayestateplanning.com. Every couple should consult a qualified estate planning attorney to assist with this important work.

In any event, I will discuss this topic in four parts:

Part 1 will address the life planning issues for gay and lesbian couples, and suggest some practical tips for same-sex couples, such as joint-ownership agreements; cohabitation agreements; buy-sell agreements for couples who have a business together; and joint-custody agreements for couples with children and prenuptial agreements.

Part 2 will address disability planning issues, such as powers of attorney; healthcare proxies; living wills; and temporary guardianship appointments. We will also discuss long-term care insurance, and other planning issues for nursing home or assisted living care.

Part 3 will address death planning issues, such as wills, trusts, and guardianship appointments for minor children. We will also discuss legal authority to deal with a body after death and the beneficiary designation selections for pension, retirement, life insurance, annuities and other beneficiary designation assets.

Part 4 will then discuss how the whether-to-wed decision factors into all of this. That is to say, what changes for estate planning documents are necessary if one gets married, and what important considerations are there from an estate planning perspective if one chooses *not* to get married.

## Part 1: Life Planning

Life events unfold. Among the most important can be finding one's life partner. This is often a happy time, and one that doesn't require the advice of counsel. But, as dating grows serious and people begin to move in together, maybe co-mingle assets, and make other life decisions that are dependent on each other's livelihood, it is important to define those obligations, and often to document them.

Let's start with the topic of a **joint-ownership agreement**. Too often, gay and lesbian couples buy property together without thinking through the exit strategy. Even if the deal is 50/50 for everything, with both parties paying half of the down payment and closing costs, and half of the ongoing maintenance and expenses, including mortgage payments, taxes and insurance, problems can arise. Without a joint-ownership agreement, particularly when the parties are not married, this can be disastrous if the relationship doesn't end well, either because the parties decide to split up, or because one of the people unexpectedly passes away.

Joint-ownership agreements can outline all of the provisions that need to be considered in these what-if scenarios, and/or in the case of sudden death. These have the effect of reducing the uncertainty for both parties and effectively protecting everyone's interest. There is not a one-size-fits-all for these agreements. A good lawyer can help you put one together. And, much like a prenuptial agreement, since both people may have different interests, it can be important for each person to be represented (or at least be able to consult with) separate lawyers.

These agreements, for instance, can provide buy-sell provisions that outline what happens in the event of a break-up, including how the property will be appraised so that a value can be set that is agreeable to both parties. This is important when one person wants to buy out the other, or when the property needs to be sold (even though one person may not really want that) to make sure true fair value is realized. They can also contain other more detailed provisions about who pays for what, and even who gets to use the property in the event of separation. They can be as detailed or as general as the parties prefer, but without them, it can really be a problem in the event of separation or death.

Like joint-ownership agreements, gay couples often enter into **co-habitation agreements (also sometimes referred to as domestic partnership agreements)**, which outline their respective obligations to each other. This can be as simple as memorializing in writing who will pay for what in terms of joint living expenses, to how income is shared, and even attempting to share retirement plan assets—although that can be tricky from a tax perspective. While doing this can create clarity for a couple (gay or straight) who live together, often life is not linear and the deal may need to change out of necessity. It is really a personal decision about whether this sort of agreement makes sense. The truth of the matter is that most couples, gay or straight, already have some sort of agreement around these issues, whether implicitly or explicitly. Reducing it to writing can help keep things clear, but can take a bit of the romance out of things.[2]

Much of the same can be said about **buy-sell agreements** when the parties enter into a business arrangement together. Often gay and lesbian couples set up small (or large) businesses and, like any family-run enterprise, it's all good until it's not. Having a written buy-sell agreement will make very clear what everyone's rights and responsibilities are, including what happens in the event of a split or death. These agreements can become complex, so they should be done with the assistance of a competent attorney. In addition, we often advise our clients to fund these agreements with life insurance on each other so that, in the event of a death, the other person's estate will have the funds to buy out the other partners. This is particularly important when the business is owned not just by a couple, but also with other parties.

**Couples with, or planning to have, children** have a host of other life planning issues to address that begin with defining and securing parental rights for both parties, if that is the intention. This topic, too, is terribly complex and varies quite a bit on a state-by-state basis. Everyone should consult a family lawyer who is knowledgeable about the issues surrounding artificial reproductive technology, and who understands the legal landscape in the state where the couple resides. But, even if you do that all correctly, remember that since state laws in this area vary quite a bit, make sure your lawyer considers what would happen if your family travels or moves to another state with different laws.

This should not be considered the sole advice on the topic, but it is increasingly common for couples who have a family by assisted reproductive technology (ART) to do a second parent adoption (if available in their state), and still enter into a joint-custody agreement, and in some instances seek court approval, so that parental rights are secured in other states as well.

The horror stories in this area abound. A lesbian couple in Ohio, for instance, wanted to start a family. Kelly Mullen and Michelle Hobbs were in a committed long-term relationship and, since they lived in a non-recognition state, were not married. They sought to have their friend Scott Liming be the sperm donor and he agreed. The parties consulted with a lawyer and did have an agreement prepared and signed that set forth their respective rights and responsibilities, including limiting his parental rights. The women, however, never set forth their obligations to one another and the child in an irrevocable joint-custody agreement, even though they had executed wills naming each other as guardian in the event of death. They even provided for each other to have decision-making authority in medical directives. So, when the relationship ended and litigation ensued, Hobbs, the non-biological mother, ultimately was denied visitation rights with the child by the Ohio Supreme Court.[3] Had a joint-custody agreement been entered into, at least under Ohio law, the result would have been different.[4]

The types of contracts that may be required can include surrogacy contracts; egg- and sperm-donor contracts; joint- or shared-custody agreements; adoption and second-parent adoption; guardianship or temporary guardianship appointments; among others.

Marriage can, in some states, lessen the need for some of these agreements. The law in most states essentially says that a child born in a marriage is presumed to be the child of both parents in that marriage. Same-sex marriage will, of course, turn this long-held legal presumption on its head, since, biologically, it is impossible for a same-sex couple to have a child without the assistance of some other person. It will take the law awhile to catch up to this reality, even in recognition states. For now, however, it is important to remember that for couples planning a family, it is critical to seek advice in this area.

Finally, **prenuptial agreements** are among the hottest topics for couples contemplating marriage, particularly if they have already been together for many years. Every couple handles money differently. Often, figuring out finances evolves over time. Basically, whenever a couple has different levels of assets (or debt) and/or different income levels, this is something that should be considered prior to marriage. Again, as with all family law matters, the rules in this area vary on a state-by-state basis. There are, however, certain common themes.

First, a prenuptial agreement, funny enough, needs to be done PRIOR to getting married. And, in many states, this includes well enough prior so that later neither party can argue duress. So, please, don't plan to sign this paperwork the hour before you go in front of your Justice of the Peace, or whomever is planning to solemnize your marriage.

Generally speaking, three criteria need to be met in order for a prenuptial agreement to be legally valid and binding:

1. Each party needs to provide full and fair financial disclosure of all assets, liability and income. Essentially, no hiding the Swiss bank account from the other, or the deal could be off.

2. Each party must be represented by separate lawyers, and some states require the lawyers to sign the agreement as well to certify that certain advice has indeed been provided.

3. Generally speaking, the agreement should be fair and reasonable at the time it is entered into, and at the time it is enforced. Here is where the case law from each state will suggest what is "fair and reasonable," and what is not.

If these conditions are met, then the prenuptial agreement will usually be presumed to be valid and legally enforceable.

So, what's typically in a prenup? While every case may be different, typically prenups address the following points (and can of course, be modified in whatever way the parties may mutually agree):

- Property (which, used here will be meant to include all assets, bank, and investment accounts, etc.) that is separately titled prior to the marriage, and that remains separately titled, will become the sole property of the owner upon divorce.

- Property that is jointly titled, or that becomes jointly titled, during the marriage will be split 50/50 upon divorce.

- Inheritances received, so long as they are kept separately titled, will remain the sole property of the owner upon divorce.

- Income is the sole property of the earner, unless otherwise agreed or placed into a joint account. This is not possible in the nine community property states: Arizona, California, Idaho, Louisiana, Nevada, New Mexico, Texas, Washington, and Wisconsin.

- Debts incurred by one remain the sole obligation of that one person, unless you live in a community property state.

- Generally speaking, and here is where it can vary a great deal depending on the circumstances of the couple, no alimony will be required of either party upon divorce.

- All issues of child custody and support are usually dealt with based on local law and often not spelled out in the prenup, unless the children are already in the picture at the time of marriage.

- Usually both parties waive their statutory right to claim the spousal elective share at death. (This is a law that exists in every state that allows a spouse to choose to take roughly 50 percent of a deceased spouse's entire estate, irrespective of what may be in his or her will or trust).

- Retirement plan assets are generally left with each party, but again can vary.

- Health insurance coverage upon divorce may be addressed.

- When a couple jointly owns real estate, sometimes the parties can decide who would get to keep the house, and whether the other one would need to be bought out, and at what terms.

Everyone getting married later in life, even if already together for some time, should at least consider doing a prenuptial agreement prior to getting married. It can be an intensely personal, and often emotional, decision for couples, so let your heart (and head) be your guide. If you choose to get married without doing one, you should also understand the consequences of that decision.

A full exposition of divorce law is beyond the scope of this book. So let it suffice to say that without a prenuptial agreement, local laws around divorce and separation of property (and alimony) will decide what happens in the event of a split. Those laws sometimes include formulas, but more often, take all the facts and circumstances of the marriage into account. What will be interesting from a same-sex marriage standpoint is to see whether the courts will take into consideration the couple's time together prior to being married. Many couples were not able to be married during many of those years, precisely because of the law. Time will tell. Generally, family law courts apply fairness principles of equity when deciding these matters.

## Part 2: Disability Planning

No one ever wants to become incapacitated. However, studies are constantly showing that we are living longer and, of course, medical technology is constantly advancing. Some believe we are more likely to have a period of incapacity before we die than we are to die prematurely, precisely because of this trend. Therefore, planning for this time, particularly when you are alive and well and are not in crisis, is important for you and your loved ones.

The planning here is pretty simple: You have to pick "back-up" people to do certain things for you in the event you become incapacitated, such as a power-of-attorney for financial matters, and an agent for making health care decisions if you cannot speak for yourself. If you are married, and live in a recognition state, these documents are slightly less necessary than they were before the changes in the law, but be careful: If you ever move, or even travel to a non-recognition state, they once again become essential. Also, what if your spouse is in the terrible accident with you, and is therefore unavailable to serve? Who will be their successor agent? I always recommend successor agents for our clients.

Indeed, for couples who travel to, or have property in, non-recognition states, we are often asked whether they need separate powers of attorney and healthcare proxies, for example, that conform to that other state's laws. The short answer is that you shouldn't have to, but you probably should do it out of an abundance of caution if you are frequently spending time in a non-recognition state. As a legal matter, each state has laws that generally recognize these agency appointments from another state, if done properly. As a practical matter, clerks in banks and nurses in hospitals are familiar with their own state forms. In the event of an emergency (which is typically when you need to produce and try to use them), you want to be able to have something that the first responder is familiar with and will readily accept. It is true that if you insist they get their general counsel's office involved to review the forms, they will likely find them to be acceptable, even if not in the form they are used to seeing in their own state. But, in order to avoid this hassle and to expedite medical care in an emergency, I sometimes suggest the "belt and suspenders" approach. I recommend doing these "ancillary" documents—such as a power of attorney and healthcare proxy (and maybe a living will)—in the form appropriate for each state where you spend considerable time, particularly if that state happens to be a non-recognition state.

Sometimes, however, even with all these good documents in place, there can be confusion when dementia, for example, sets in. When should they be used? Who decides whether someone is actually incompetent? Every state has a court-supervised process for this, typically called a guardianship proceeding, where with proper evidence and a court process, a judge can decide this. If, however, you want to ensure more control over this process than turning it over to an unknown judge, you can draft for it in your estate planning documents, so that it is decided privately by people you know and trust. Often this is called a disability panel.

Years ago, trusts used to typically say, "Any two licensed physicians can determine that I am incompetent by certifying in writing . . ." Our approach is to suggest that you have someone you know and trust weighing in on the decision with, perhaps, a doctor or two. Our disability panels usually consist of a spouse or partner with the primary care or attending physician, and then a back-up for the spouse if he or she is unavailable. This is usually a trusted family member or friend. A knowledgeable estate planning lawyer can help you figure out what makes the most sense given your personal situation.

Another aspect of disability planning includes planning for long-term care needs, either in an assisted-living situation or a nursing home. I've never met anyone who really wants to go into such a facility, but sometimes there are no other choices. Since Medicare does not cover the costs associated with long-term care in either assisted-living facilities or nursing homes, the single best way to plan for this, from an economic perspective, is to work with a financial expert who understands long-term care insurance. These policies can be tricky and have changed in recent years. Some policies cover in-home care needs, and others simply pay a certain daily rate. Some are indexed for inflation, and others are not. Some require a waiting period or co-pay, and others do not. Again, it's complex, and an expert can help you evaluate your options in this area. Doing it sooner—meaning at a younger age—means it will be less expensive, as these policies become very expensive as we age. In addition, they often become unavailable if we are too old, or worse yet—if we get the horrible diagnosis. So, if it is something you're concerned about, run the numbers with an expert.

If LTC insurance is not an option, then some people do what is called "Medicaid planning." This is also sometimes referred to as elder law, and was discussed in Chapter 4. This is a way to protect your assets—usually at least your home—so that if nursing home care becomes necessary, then perhaps you could become eligible for governmental benefits to cover the costs and protect your assets for your spouse and loved ones.

Medicaid planning is another tricky area of law. In some respects, being married helps here, and in others, it may not.

First, with respect to the home: a well spouse (meaning legally married and living in a recognition state) will never be forced to leave the home if the unwell spouse needs nursing home care and can't pay for it. Instead, assuming the unwell spouse qualifies for the governmental benefits of Medicaid, the well spouse can remain in the home for his or her life and never be forced to move or sell the home. However, during this same period, if the unwell spouse is receiving benefits from Medicaid, a lien will be accruing and attached to the home. This means that after both spouses are gone, Medicaid gets paid back BEFORE any other heirs can collect proceeds from the sale of the home. So, this can be both good news and bad news.

So, what can be done about this? Well, people often set up irrevocable trusts for the benefit of each other, first, and then for their ultimate heirs. They put the house, and sometimes other assets, into this type of trust. It is also sometimes known as a Medicaid trust. If these were easy to set up, everyone would simply do this just before (and only if) they needed nursing home care. The federal government has put tight restrictions on these types of trusts, however. Since federal Medicaid programs are administered by the states, every state's rules in this area are slightly different.

As a general matter, the main rules are:

1. In order for one or both people in the couple to become eligible for Medicaid, they essentially both need to be poor. The rules for asset and income tests are strict and vary state by state, but it is often the case that the unwell spouse can only have $1,000 or $2,000 total in his or her name and the well spouse can only have $110,000 (or so, but that number varies and changes) of countable assets. IRA assets are countable in some states and not in others. There are a host of rules around what is "countable" for purposes of these limits.

2. The assets in the trust will not be counted toward these limits unless two conditions are met: first, the trust needs to have been set up and "funded"—meaning property put into these trusts—generally **five years** prior to seeking coverage by Medicaid; and, second the trust can provide **income-only** access to the primary beneficiaries. This means there is no access to the principle by the married couple. This is relatively easy when it comes to a home, since living in it is the "income," and the "principle" is the equity in the home once it is sold. However, for all other assets— such as bank accounts, retirement assets, savings and investment accounts—they are all considered "countable" assets. And, it is important to note that they are counted for both people, if the couple is married. This then can be a downside of being married.

This is a highly complex area of the law and, as my friends say, you should "not try this at home alone!" Consult a Medicaid or an elder law attorney, if this is something you are concerned about.

## Part 3: Death Planning

Some of my favorite comments from clients are: "I'm not planning to die anytime soon." And, "If I die. . ." The truth of the matter is, sooner or later we all go, and planning for this inevitable event is better (for your loved ones) than not planning for it.

Not planning for death can be okay if you don't mind how long it takes for people to get access to your assets, or even where they may wind up. Every state has intestacy laws that prescribe a set of rules for what happens to people's property when they die without a will or trust. Those processes, I like to say, are the Full-Employment Act for the lawyers. "Intestacy probate," which is probate without a will, takes more time and costs more money than it would to create and execute estate planning documents. In other words, by doing proper estate planning, your loved one's (when grieving) will have an easier time paying bills and having access to funds to continue to live as you would hope.

With probate (which is necessary with or without a will, and only unnecessary if you have set up and funded trusts, which we will discuss in a bit), certain notices need to be sent, usually to a long list of blood relatives. Sometimes notices to creditors need to be published in local papers, and bond often must be purchased to secure the obligations of the estate by the personal representative (which is the modern term for executor). In short, with intestacy probate, there are a host of hurdles to jump through that take time and cost money.

Some people who think they are clever try to do estate planning by avoiding lawyers and documents at all costs. This sometimes works. If you title your property jointly and make all your accounts joint, and you make sure you have beneficiary designations filled out on all retirement plans and annuities, then by operation of title, your property can pass to the surviving joint owner, or named beneficiary, and you can, indeed, avoid probate with respect to those assets.

But, be sure to cooperate and die in order. Meaning, if your partner or spouse is the named beneficiary or joint account owner, make sure he or she is never in the same car or plane with you, because, if the awful thing happens when you're together, then this form of plan can quickly fall apart at the seams. The worst consequence to this type of planning is when things (meaning assets or property) go sideways and don't end up where you intend. Let me give you an example.

Let's assume (God forbid) that my husband and I are in the same car crash and I am instantly killed, but he survives for six months (in a coma). If we had set up our plan as indicated above, everything in joint name, all of my property would pass to him and, assuming he never had an opportunity to do his own will or trust, his property would pass to his surviving "heirs-at-law." This is usually someone's closest biological relatives, such as children, parents or siblings. It could even be nieces or nephews, or aunts and uncles, etc. In our case, it would be his parents and brother. But, what about my parents, brother and sisters? They would be out of luck. Everything would go "sideways." Not that I don't love my in-laws, but this is not what either of us would ever have intended.

Instead, what is always best is a proper estate plan that considers all of the scenarios and has some "what-if" provisions baked in. A well-thought-out and drafted estate plan can address all of these issues. What's more, it can provide flexibility to have cascading beneficiaries in place after both of you are gone.

Go back to my example. Let's say I want to leave everything to my husband, but if he doesn't use it all up, I want the balance of what's left to go to my nieces and nephew, and maybe some of my favorite charities. We can do this pretty easily by setting up a revocable living trust (RLT) that lists him first as the sole beneficiary of a marital trust, and later my relatives (not his) as the ultimate beneficiaries of that trust. This type of trust-based planning can be effective as well for unmarried couples, but without some of the state and federal estate tax advantages that are afforded to spouses.

Now this may not be the plan for everyone, but the trust vehicle usually provides more flexibility to ensure that you can have cascading beneficiaries beyond each other. It also, if properly done, can ensure that nothing reverts to the state after you are both gone! The best feature of a revocable living trust, however, is that it can avoid all of the probate hassles, if it is properly set up and funded during your lifetime. Funding a trust is simply the process of re-titling assets into the name of the trust. This often includes changing the deed to your home, and sometimes, changing retirement plan and life insurance beneficiaries to name the trust instead of a person. With this process, you still maintain control of your property while you're alive and well, since you would name yourself as the lifetime trustee. But, you would also need to name successor trustees upon disability and death to take over the management of your affairs. By fully funding your trust, you can avoid the time-consuming and costly court processes of probate.

## Part 4: How Marriage Affects Estate Planning

If one chooses to get married for all the reasons outlined in prior chapters, then estate planning documents will need to be updated. Indeed, in some states, a prior will or trust becomes legally invalid just by virtue of getting married. There is often an assumption in the law that one should change one's will or trust to make sure to provide for the new spouse.

In any event, there can be important tax planning reasons to update your documents as a result of marriage. As I've explained already, some states have a state estate tax that could apply. The federal government has one as well. For couples living in a recognition state, those state and federal estate taxes do not apply to married same-sex couples now. However, in order to optimize the amount of your estate that passes to anyone other than a spouse, and minimize taxes, it is important to establish certain types of trusts that are often referred to as family and marital trusts.*

These trusts, if properly done, can have the effect of not only receiving the full marital deduction upon death (no estate tax for a U.S. citizen surviving spouse**), but they can also optimize the amount of assets that others receive after the second spouse passes. This is particularly important for couples with children. In addition, if properly done, these trusts can allow each spouse to inherit from the other with some protections on the

---

* There are other names for these trusts, like credit shelter and QTIP or A/B trusts, but—whatever they are called—they are the classic tax planning trusts for married couples

** Non-citizen spouses can inherit without estate taxes as well, but only if a certain kind of trust is established called a qualified domestic trust under specific rules issued by the IRS.

inheritance. What kind of protections? Well, let's say the surviving spouse, in a weak moment, meets "Betty-the-Barmaid," or "Bo-the-Tennis-Pro" (depending on your preference), and gets remarried. Then, if that subsequent marriage turns out to have been a bad idea, Betty or Bo may wind up with a considerable amount of your assets that you had intended for your surviving spouse, not their bimbo. With proper trust planning, you can put re-marriage protections in for the inheritance. There are other protections, such as asset protections for lawsuits, for example, if the surviving spouse may be in a high-risk profession, such as a surgeon or OB-GYN doctor.

For couples who may be subject to a state estate tax, there are other planning techniques that are also available. A good estate planning lawyer can, for sure, help you on this.

One practical suggestion I always make is to check the definitions in the documents to make sure that the definition of spouse includes the spouse in any state where the will or trust may be administered, whether or not that state recognizes the marriage at the time of such administration. In addition, we usually include a definition of children (or "issue" or "descendants") that includes all children born to, or adopted by, parents in a lawful marriage—even if another state would not recognize them. A knowledgeable estate planning lawyer can help you with these custom clauses.

One last word of caution: For those who may stand to inherit property or assets from parents or other older family members (such as grandparents, or aunts or uncles), make sure they, too, update their estate plan documents with similar expansive definitions. If they are in a non-recognition state and thought they were including your spouse or children in the inheritance, they may not be unless it is properly and carefully drafted.

If you are the fortunate beneficiary of family trusts that were long ago set up and included "spouse" or "children" ("issue" or "descendants") as named beneficiaries, and if there is confusion or debate with the trustee about whether this applies to your family—consult a good lawyer! Sometimes the trust can be removed to a "friendly" (recognition) state so as to be included as a beneficiary. The complexities of this are beyond the scope of what I can cover here, but if this situation applies to you, definitely ask about decanting with your estate lawyer.

# CHAPTER 9

# Unique Issues Related to Marriage for Bisexual, Transgender, Gay Elder and Youth Communities

There are a host of issues not previously discussed that may profoundly affect other members of the LGBT community. Not all of them relate to marriage; but some do. The LGBT community cannot easily be put into a box. While I have discussed many of the legal issues relating to gay and lesbian couples, there are several members of our community that will face challenges, legal uncertainty, and outright discrimination as they lead their lives. This chapter is only meant to highlight these challenges. The challenges these members of our community face are often highly localized and intensely personal.

## Bisexual

Couples where one or both identifies as bisexual have a clear legal and tax course to follow if they are opposite gender, and the same issues as same-sex couples if they are of the same gender with respect to marriage rights and benefits. In this respect, the legal and tax analysis is simple. There are other emotional and social attitudes that can create complexities, however. Those are beyond the scope of this book. While the social issues for bisexual people may be different (and I do not mean to dismiss them), the legal and tax issues related to whether to wed are essentially the same as those mentioned already in this book, to the extent that the couple are of the same gender. Therefore, if a couple is of opposite gender—bisexual or otherwise—there are no material legal or tax differences for that couple to contemplate (and benefit from) being married. If the couple is of the same gender, then they will face all of the same issues already discussed for same-sex couples.

The bisexual community, however, does face important other issues related to marriage generally. It is a specialized world, and one that deserves experts to address the specific social and emotional issues. I have identified here a few resources for those individuals and couples where one or both identify as bisexual and are discussing the challenges and rewards of marriage:

> www.biresources.net
> www.bisexual.org
> www.binetusa.org

## Transgender

The complexities faced by the transgender community cannot be overstated. There are large social issues around discrimination, access to quality healthcare, and acceptance of gender identity and expression. The complexities around gender identity and expression are also complex, but I will limit this discussion to the legal issues facing individuals who are transgender.

There are several factors related to marriage that transgender individuals and couples will need to consider. Some couples will have to face the issue of should they get married prior to one (or both) of the members of the couple transitioning. Other challenges are presented in a relationship when one of the members of the couple transitions after a marriage.

Couples concerned about the legal issues raised by marriage should consult an attorney or resource center that specializes in transgender law. It is highly complex and specialized. As a general matter, no court or legislature has yet adopted rules that could extinguish a valid marriage by virtue of a gender transition. The general rule is that marriage can only be extinguished by divorce dissolution or death. Thus, a gender transition after marriage that turns an opposite-sex couple into a same-sex married couple will not invalidate the marriage, even in non-recognition states.

However, if the transition from a same-sex couple into an opposite sex couple occurs after the marriage, depending on the state, the marriage may continue to be viewed as a same-sex marriage. Or it might even become an invalid marriage, if it was performed in a non-recognition state and the officiants did not realize the parties were of the same-sex at the time they entered into their union. In this situation, it is possible that the marriage will not be recognized in any of the non-recognition states. That is what we have recently seen from a case in Texas.[1] Here Nikki Araguz, born male and named Justin Purdue at birth, married Thomas Araguz in Texas in 2008 and transitioned to female shortly after the marriage. She had her birth certificate changed to identify her as female at birth, and of course, she also legally changed her name. After her husband, Thomas, a firefighter, was killed in the line of duty, she applied for certain widow benefits. Thomas' mother and ex-wife brought a challenge claiming the marriage should not be recognized since Texas does not recognize same-sex marriages. They said the benefits should go to the children from his prior marriage instead. So far, the Texas courts have sided with the mother and ex-wife, not the widow, and the case is on appeal.[2]

This same case presents the other interesting conundrum of whether gender transition can create an opposite sex couple for legal marriage in a non-recognition state. Here, Nikki sought marriage to another man and was first denied a marriage license by one county clerk in Texas, yet another issued the license. Since Nikki Araguz is an avowed activist, it is likely we have not heard the last of this case yet.

Texas notwithstanding, we are starting to see some changes that will have positive outcomes for transgender couples at the federal level. Just recently, the Social Security Administration has made it easier for individuals to change their gender identity in the Social Security Database.[3]

We are starting to see societal and legal advances for the transgender community, generally, that may over time influence the important marriage rights. Recently, we have seen greater protections and acceptance for transgender students. The Equal Employment Opportunity Commission (EEOC) has recently ruled that Title VII, which applies to sex discrimination, also applies to transgender employees. While these are minor advances for the community as a whole, they still leave challenges for couples in relation to marriage. There is some case law out there on these questions,[4] but this will be a continuing and evolving area of the law.

There are also terrific resources out there for more in-depth analysis and assistance for people in this community. Check out the resources at:

www.tgctr.org
www.transgenderlawcenter.org
www.transgenderlaw.org

## Elders

Our elders, straight, gay or otherwise, are increasingly the forgotten ones in our modern American society. Many Americans hope to age at home, but sometimes they simply can't. The current generation of gay and lesbian elders are less likely to have children to take care of them in their old age. Increasingly, as these elders seek assisted living support, they are finding discrimination anew, and are needing to sometimes go back into the closet to survive in these environments.

The best treatment of these issues, second to none, is Professor Nancy Knauer's work: *Gay and Lesbian Elders: History, Law and Identity Politics in the United States.*[5] This book is highly recommended for further exploration and understanding of the broader issues affecting the elder LGBT community in the United States today.

In terms of whether to wed, one of the biggest issues gay elders face is whether marriage would put them in a better or worse position for planning for, and paying for, nursing home care, if that becomes necessary.

No one ever wants to go into a nursing home. It is, however, necessary in a variety of circumstances. Costs are high, and growing, and can devastate a family's life savings. In order to address this, a whole new area of law has emerged called elder law, or Medicaid planning, which we have discussed in earlier chapters. In any event, the issue in this area is how to qualify the "unwell" spouse—while keeping assets available for the well spouse. The techniques involved often include the use of irrevocable (income only) trusts and sometimes annuities and other strategies. Medicaid, like SSI (Supplemental Security Income), is a means-tested benefit, which means that the assets of both parties in a married couple are counted in order to determine whether one is eligible.

At first blush, therefore, you may think that getting married later in life, if one person is likely to need nursing home care, might not be a good idea. Indeed, there are even stories of elders needing to get divorced in order to qualify. However, at least some attorneys in the elder law area with whom I have consulted don't agree.

They believe there are more planning options available to a married couple than a single person. Each case is different, and it really will depend on the level of assets in each person's name, income and other factors. This is another area where you really need to consult an elder law attorney to discuss your personal situation and see whether it makes sense, from a planning perspective, to get married.

Another big issue for gay elders is being able to protect the surviving partner or spouse, so that he/she can remain in the home after one is gone. Marriage provides considerable benefits that even a properly done will or trust may not.

For sure, a surviving partner is completely exposed when an unmarried couple doesn't have any estate plan documents in place. Frank Vasquez learned this the hard way after his partner of twenty-eight years, Robert Schwerzler, died in 2001. The home and cars were titled in Robert's name, so after he passed away, his siblings became the lawful heirs to his property under Washington state law, and literally tried to put Frank out on the street with nothing.[6] This story, unlike many others, actually had a moderately happy ending. While Robert's family tried to argue in the court case that Frank was merely a housekeeper and boarder, and that their late brother was not gay, the Washington Supreme Court used an equitable theory of adoption to award the entire estate to Frank, but only after years of litigation.[7]

This story underscores the need to have some legal recognition of a relationship, and to do proper estate planning. Had the couple been married, or even registered as domestic partners, Frank would have had more legal rights upon Robert's death. Of course, had they done proper estate planning—particularly living trusts which were funded during their lifetimes—all of this could have been avoided. (Funding is the process of retitling assets into the trust, like the deed to the house and bank and investment accounts, as well as changing beneficiary designation forms to name the trust as a beneficiary. With respect to beneficiary forms, there are tricky tax issues involved here, and a professional advisor should be consulted before making those changes.)

Marriage matters, especially for elderly couples who want to ensure that their surviving partner has strong legal rights to inherit property, particularly the family home, after one is gone.

Finally, another issue we sadly see with elders has to do with those who, for whatever reason, chose to remain in the closet their entire lives and now may be "outed" at death as a way for their partner or spouse to inherit property. Professor Knauer, in her book on gay and lesbian elders, tells the story of two lesbians who lived their lives together secretly for thirty-two years.[8] When Ms. H died, leaving her entire estate to her life partner, Ms. F, the challenges began. Ms. H's family claimed "undue influence," and even forgery of the will, to stop the inheritance. While the case ultimately settled, and Ms. F did receive the house and one-third of the estate, it is clear that if they had been married, or at least had done trust-based planning with full lifetime funding, the result would likely have been different.

These issues need to be carefully navigated with the help of good advisors. Marriage can, for sure, help protect the survivor at least with respect to the rights to inherit property.

There are also many great national LGBT organizations out there that provide specific support and resources to the elder gay community including:

> www.sageusa.org
> www.lgbtagingproject.org
> www.lgbtagingcenter.org
> www.gleh.org
> www.oloc.org

There are also a variety of smaller local and regional organizations focused on the elderly LGBT population.

## Youth

Lastly, I would be remiss if I did not mention the youth culture. Ever changing and vibrant, we now see more "out" kids than ever before. Schools are increasingly embracing LGBTQ groups—including those who are "questioning" in the middle school and high school years, as well as in college.

In this author's humble opinion, marriage should not be on this demographic's radar screen yet. They are too young. There are, however, age restrictions in most states about how old a person must be before being able to marry. In some states, below certain ages, marriage may be permitted with parental consent.

In any event, the issues are not entirely different than those discussed in earlier chapters. Some issues, however, that might be unique to this group are those related to student loan eligibility. Qualification for these loans, whether under a federal program, state or private institution, will vary somewhat. But, as a general matter, they all require the applicant to disclose, and the lending party to consider, the income and assets of the family. If you're married, that will include the income and assets of your spouse (and not your parents).

Generally, student debt belongs to the individual student, unless another party, such as a spouse, co-signed, in which case they would have joint liability for the debt. These debts are extinguished at death, so they would not need to be assumed by a surviving spouse.

# CHAPTER 10

# Finding LGBT-Savvy Advisors

Finding qualified advisors to help navigate this area can be surprisingly difficult, particularly depending on what part of the country you live in. While most major cities and metropolitan areas tend to have more gay and gay-friendly lawyers, CPAs and financial advisors, not all of them actually understand the technical issues in this area as well as they should. Indeed, in the last few years, many large financial institutions have begun marketing heavily to the LGBT community. It has become a lucrative demographic, previously ignored by these large firms, and many are now eagerly trying to capture market share.

While on one level, it is a good thing that we are now accepted, even sought after, by mainstream banks and investment firms, it can be dangerous, too. It's one thing to be okay with the "gay thing." It's quite another to understand the technical issues and personal dynamics that make planning for us different. Some firms have done a better job than others in ramping up the learning curve around these technical issues. Those are the ones you want to find.

In fact, there is a recent designation offered by the college for financial planning called Accredited Domestic Partnership Advisor$^{SM}$, or ADPA®. This certification requires an advisor to study and accomplish a certain level of mastery of the unique issues same-sex couples now face in financial planning. It is a graduate-level program designed to cover the financial planning needs of same-sex couples, and it includes review of issues faced by heterosexual couples who have chosen not to marry, but who want to plan their financial lives together. Specifically covered are factors and situations that cause financial planning for domestic partners to be different from financial planning for legally married spouses. It also includes a review of same-sex married couple issues in both recognition and non-recognition states, including wealth transfer, taxation, retirement planning, and estate planning issues, as well as alternative planning solutions for these situations.

In order to be eligible for the ADPA program, advisors must currently hold one of the following designations or certifications: CRPC®, AAMS®, AWMA®, APMA®, CIMA, ChFC, JD, CPA, CFA, CTFA, or CFP®.[1]

If a financial advisor has the ADPA designation, he or she is more likely to have worked with the gay community and have spent time and energy learning the technical areas that differ for gay couples, and can help navigate these tricky waters.

Unfortunately, there are not (yet, at least) similar designations for CPAs or attorneys. Here, I recommend you evaluate these advisors on the following criteria, in no particular order of importance:

1. Are they members of any LGBT professional groups—where they will likely have attended seminars (or even taught some) on the technical issues facing our community? For lawyers, this would include a local LGBT bar association, or the national LBGT Bar Association.

2. Do they speak or write on the topic? There is an old adage: "The best way to learn something is to teach it." If your advisor has given a course, workshop, lecture or written an article (or a book!) on some topic related to planning with the LGBT community, they likely know what they're talking about, and are better prepared

than the average advisor to counsel you on these highly technical issues.

3. Does their website reference this aspect of their practice? Many advisors with whom this author speaks ask the question: "How can I market to the gay community?" Marketing to the gay community is one thing; being out and proud about working with us is quite another. Check out their website and see what content and/or references to planning within the gay community you find there.

4. Do they have a person or practice group truly dedicated to doing this work? One way to find this out is to check out their website. If they do, they will tell you.[2]

5. Ask whether they have worked with same-sex couples, and if so, how many? It is perfectly okay to ask for client references. While all advisors are bound by confidentiality provisions, and could not give references without asking their client's permission, they can ask and, if they have happy and satisfied clients, they will likely get permission for you to speak with them.

Understand, too, how the advisor is compensated. If you are dealing with a financial advisor, find out if they do "fee-only" planning, meaning they will work with you to put a plan together, whether or not you move assets under management with them. Or, do they only provide advice if you purchase a product from them (like an annuity or long-term care insurance policy), or move money under their management, such as an IRA rollover? If it's the latter, then find out how those fees work. Some money managers charge based on the total assets under management—and it's a percentage of the total. Others charge a fee up-front for each product sold—like front-end fees on mutual funds. Still others are paid by the vendor of the product, so it comes off the top when you, for example, set up an annuity.

No one works for free, nor should they. However, everyone should understand how their advisor is being compensated and be comfortable with it. Sometimes, advice can be skewed a bit based on the compensation model. Our best advice in this area is to have an open and frank discussion with your advisor about this. If you can't, then you have the wrong advisor.

Lawyers and accountants typically charge either on an hourly basis, or a fixed-fee based on the size, complexity and scope of a project. Increasingly, for example, estate-planning packages are done on a fixed-fee basis. Be sure to inquire what is included and not included. For example, here is a list of questions everyone should ask any estate-planning attorney:

1. If you are suggesting setting up a trust-based estate plan, will you help to fund the trusts? If so, is that included in the fees quoted? If not, what are the fees to do so?

2. How often should we update our plan documents, and what is the fee to do that?

3. How much would you charge to administer this estate after I am gone? Is there any way to control those costs?

4. Will you be able to help me/us locate other allied professional advisors, like a CPA and/or financial advisor who understand our situation? Do you get referral fees from that?

5. Who will I actually be dealing with if I sign up with your firm/company? Who will do the work?

6. What if I am not satisfied with the process or results?

7. What problems have you had with other clients and how have you resolved them?

At the end of the day, you have to trust your advisors, since you will be dealing with intensely personal information. Go with your gut; it's usually right.

# CHAPTER 11

# What Next for Same-Sex Marriage and Whether to Wed?

While it's always dangerous to predict the future—my crystal ball is no clearer than anyone else's—here are some thoughts about what the future may hold for the legal recognition of same-sex marriages in the United States.

For sure, there will be more court cases. There are already dozens around the United States at the time of this writing that challenge both the "min-DOMAs" in a number of states, and one state's non-recognition of another state's (valid) same-sex marriage. The federal court cases working their way up to the U.S. Supreme Court deal with the fundamental constitutional issue of whether there is a right by same-sex couples to be married under the U.S. Constitution. The legal theories here are plentiful, and we won't attempt to do them justice, but by way of summary, the arguments include those under due process and equal protection—two powerful constitutional law theories.

Some legal scholars have suggested that another avenue for challenges may be the "full faith and credit" clause of the U.S. Constitution. Since this clause only applies to judgments from other states, its application here may be limited. That said, it is possible that a couple from a non-recognition state could get married in a recognition state, and before returning home, seek some sort of declaratory judgment about their marriage. If this were to happen and the home (non-recognition) state refused to recognize that order or judgment, then it is possible that the couple could bring a challenge under this other legal theory too.

The opposition theories starting to emerge are also interesting. They sometimes have to do with our First Amendment's guarantee of freedom of religion. Under this theory, opponents to same-sex marriage will argue that forcing any state to recognize same-sex marriages infringes on people's freedom of religion because it is contrary to their religious beliefs. While it may sound like a stretch, it is a powerful argument in some parts of the country, and it is gaining momentum.[1]

Two cases that many in the advocacy world seem to be watching closely as potentially the next ones to go to the Supreme Court are two cases from the Ninth Circuit—one from Nevada, and another from Hawaii.[2] Both seek to find a constitutional right for same-sex couples to be married.

Some lawyers close to the movement have suggested that the case from Nevada may be the next one to get to Supreme Court. But there are others to watch. The well-known legal team of conservative Republican lawyer Theodore Olson and liberal Democrat David Boies have recently joined forces again in a federal court case in Virginia challenging that state's ban of legal recognition on every level for same-sex couples on federal constitutional grounds.[3] (Olson and Boies first faced off in the famous *Bush v. Gore* battle at the Supreme Court over the presidential election in 2000 and later became a powerful team in the California gay marriage case that was the other one before the Supreme Court in June 2013—*Hollingsworth v. Perry.*)

Another case to watch that may become a basis for review by the Supreme Court is one from Pennsylvania. There a same-sex couple who married in Massachusetts in 2005 and relocated to Pennsylvania later that same year so one in the couple could accept a post-doctoral fellowship at Bryn Mawr College. That couple has brought suit challenging Pennsylvania's position of not recognizing their marriage and declaring it "void" for all state law purposes, having the effect of requiring them to go through a multistep process so both could become the legal parent of their child. Cara Palladino and Isabelle Barker (the former post-grad student) brought this suit, naming Governor Tom Corbett as the defendant (Palladino v. Corbett)[4] in what some have reported could be the "Most Ingenious Attack on Gay Marriage Bans."[5] In *Windsor*, Justice Kennedy, writing for the majority, in striking down section 3 of DOMA, said that Congress could not single out a class of persons deemed by a state entitled to recognition and protection. Kennedy went on to say in that opinion that, "no legitimate purpose overcomes the purpose and effect to disparage those who the State, by its marriage laws, sought to protect in personhood and dignity." So, one might wonder, if Congress can't do that—then what makes Pennsylvania think they can? Stay tuned. . .

There are, however, over thirty cases now working their way through the courts of appeal on their way up to the Supreme Court. If the Hawaii, Nevada, Virginia, Pennsylvania or any of these other cases are heard in the near term, and depending on what is decided, it could have sweeping ramifications for the equal marriage movement in the United States. Until then, we will continue to have a "patchwork" effect of the law. And, if we lose, the patchwork will likely remain for a considerably longer time.

It is entirely possible, however, that any one of these next cases may come up too soon and set the equal marriage movement back for decades if there were a loss. Legal commentator, Tom Goldstein, on SCOTUSBLOG, an authoritative source for analyzing Supreme Court happenings and cases recently suggested:

> *"But the moments at which justice seems within reach can present social movements with their greatest tests. The Court's recent rulings have lit a fuse that may have a bomb at the other end. Individual couples who have misread the signals from the Supreme Court instead launched much broader constitutional challenges to the traditional definition of marriage."[6]*

In this same posting, Goldstein suggests that, while the Supreme Court may "duck" the first one or two of these cases currently on appeal, eventually, it will likely take up the question of whether there is a federal constitutional right of same-sex couples to be married. If the Court decides negatively on this question, Goldstein suggests it would stall the trend toward full recognition, and leave marriage laws for each state to separately decide. This would perpetuate the confusion by the patchwork effect discussed at length in this book.

Until the Supreme Court decides otherwise, there will continue to be recognition states and non-recognition states, and those will continue to change over time. (For updates on the changing landscape of recognition and non-recognition states, see the map of the United States regularly updated on the Human Rights Campaign website: www.hrc.org.) We will also continue to have the overlay of the federal government's position of whether it will recognize marriages for certain purposes of federal benefits based on either place of domicile or place of celebration. This, too, will likely change and evolve as private parties launch court challenges to the regulations that are issued by each agency.

For instance, a lower court in New Jersey recently ruled that in light of the *Windsor* case, the state's civil union law no longer adequately provides equal rights to same-sex couples in the state because the federal government's marriage rights don't extend to civil unions. That court ruled that denying same-sex couples the right to marry in New Jersey now violates the state constitution under its principles of equal protection under the law.[7] The Garden State case is interesting in that it would be the first state court to rule its non-recognition status unconstitutional based on the Supreme Court's holding in *Windsor*. Here, the New Jersey court basically found that because certain federal benefits were only available to same-sex couples based on marriage and not civil unions, that the New Jersey civil union law is insufficient to provide equality to those citizens and therefore violates the state's equal protection clause of the state constitution. Examples cited in the case were federal employees living and working in New Jersey who were not eligible now to participate in the federal pension system, since they were not able to become married in New Jersey.

The New Jersey history of civil unions is interesting, and this case and its history may affect many other non-recognition states. New Jersey's highest court, in 2006, found that same-sex couples should have all the same rights and benefits of a married couple, but stopped short of requiring marriage to become available to them. This is similar to what the Vermont Supreme Court had done earlier. The effect of this decision was to require the state legislature to fashion a solution, which they did by adopting what became their civil union statute. This law gave all the same rights and benefits of marriage to same-sex couples, except for the name (and of course, the fact that such rights didn't extend to the federal benefits was moot at the time, since DOMA was alive and well when that law was past).

But, once the federal government became obligated to recognize same-sex marriage for federal benefit purposes, all of the sudden, these same couples in New Jersey no longer had all the same rights and benefits of their straight counterparts in New Jersey, because the federal benefits flow based on marriage alone, and not based on other quasi-marriage rights. (In addition to the federal worker pension benefits, for example, are all the federal tax rights that now flow based on marriage, and specifically exclude other same-sex legal recognition forms, such as civil unions.)

The New Jersey Supreme Court cleared the way for same-sex marriages to begin as early as October 21, 2013. The higher court ruled that the lower court decision's order should not be "stayed" pending appeal since it found that continuing to deny same-sex couples the right to marry would cause irreparable harm. In that same opinion, the court also suggested that the appeal was not likely to be successful. Governor Chris Christie, who already vetoed a gay marriage bill that passed the legislature, announced he will no longer seek an appeal of this lower court ruling essentially securing equal marriage rights now in the Garden State and making it the fourteenth recognition state in the union.

While the proverbial "sausage" continues to be made in this area, we will have the overlay of the conflict of law and choice of law issues to navigate around. This is a highly technical area of the law in which sometimes people living in one state may choose the laws of another state to govern, for example, certain estate plan documents. We have increasingly seen, for example, couples from Virginia (a particularly hostile state for same-sex marriage rights) come to a place like Massachusetts, which is more gay friendly, to not only get married, but sometimes to do their estate planning, and set up trusts, here as well. They often choose a local resident as co-trustee, and do certain other things to have sufficient "contacts" with the jurisdiction, so that they can then have their trusts governed by Massachusetts law instead of Virginia. This, if it works, could provide considerable protections for the couple who return to live and maybe die in a place like Virginia, where for now, their relationship is not recognized by that state on any level.

This is a tricky and complicated area of the law, and same-sex couples are advised to consult a qualified attorney to help them navigate these issues.

Whether you decide to wed or not—for all of the important legal, tax, and financial planning considerations outlined herein—is, of course, a very personal decision. Even if you live in a state where the recognition may be limited for now, what we always tell clients is that if you want to be able to claim the rights that all Americans have as a married couple, then you have to be married to make that claim. Some couples waited for the federal recognition; others are still waiting for their states to recognize the right. The risk in waiting is that the awful thing could happen to one of you, and then it's too late to get married. If one person in a long-standing and committed relationship dies suddenly, the surviving partner is left with a host of issues to deal with, including some of the legal, tax and financial ones addressed here. If the law then catches up and rights are recognized, it would be too late to get married if one person has passed away.

I will conclude with my top ten questions everyone should consider when contemplating whether to wed:

1. Where do we want to live now and in the future? If full marriage recognition rights are important to you, on a state level, moving to or retiring in a non-recognition state may give you pause.

2. What effect will our marriage have on our income tax situation?

3. What effect will our marriage have on our employment benefits, if any?

4. What effect will our marriage have on our retirement savings plan (and/or pension) benefits?

5. Would marriage put us in a better estate tax position?

6. Is getting married enough? If we live in a quasi-marriage state, should we also register as domestic partners, or enter into a civil union?

7. What needs to change in our health care and estate plan documents if we do get married?

8. Will marriage put us in a better or worse position for nursing home cost coverage and other long-term care needs?

9. How will marriage affect us if we live in or travel to non-recognition states?

10. What happens if we break up? Can we get divorced, or would we need to travel or move to do that?

The legal, tax and financial issues surrounding same-sex marriage are complex. Analyzing them properly for yourself and your partner is likely something that warrants good professional help. In many ways, while landmark court cases, such as *Goodridge* and *Windsor*, have opened a whole new world of possibilities for gay and lesbian couples in ways that many never imagined possible, they have also opened a Pandora's box of tricky legal and tax issues that need to be carefully navigated. These issues will change and evolve as the laws and regulations continue to change and new cases are decided by the courts, including, likely the Supreme Court.

While this book has focused on the legal and tax issues surrounding same-sex marriage, there are also many emotional and personal issues associated with "tying-the-knot." My advice is to separate this question of whether to wed into two buckets: First, find the best legal, tax and financial advisors available. Work with them to think logically and objectively through the technical issues and the ramifications of marriage. And, then, last, but not least, take the time to really listen to your heart, and each other, and figure out what matters most for you as a couple. Sometimes, it's not always just about taxes. . .

And finally, as William Shakespeare so famously wrote, "to thine own self be true." (William Shakespeare, Hamlet, Act 1, Scene 3)

# Addendum:
## More Recognition States

As noted earlier in this book, the trend toward more states adopting marriage equality is clear. Since this book was finished, there continues to be progress on this front. Illinois is now poised to become the fifteenth state to recognize same-sex marriage, after the state legislature passed a bill on November 5, 2013. Governor Pat Quinn has stated he intends to sign it into law on November 20, 2013, with an effective date of June 1, 2014. This would allow same-sex marriages to begin on June 2, 2014 after the mandatory one-day waiting period. When Illinois joins ranks with other recognition states, 37 percent of the population in the United States will live in a state that recognizes same-sex marriage.

Hawaii, where in many respects this very public debate began some twenty years ago, is also poised to join the ranks of recognition states. On November 8, 2013, its House of Representatives finally passed a same-sex marriage bill after much debate. This bill was modified somewhat from the version already passed by the state Senate. Governor Neil Abercrombie is expected to sign that bill into law with an effective date perhaps even before that of Illinois' law, making these two states the fifteenth and sixteenth recognition states in the Union.

There are even more to come, including perhaps New Mexico, currently the only state that does not recognize or prohibit same-sex marriages. Eight counties currently issue marriage licenses to same-sex couples in New Mexico, and the state Supreme Court heard oral arguments on October 23, 2013 in a case that could resolve it once and for all. A decision is expected any time now. Opponents, however, are already organizing a ballot initiative if same-sex marriage is approved by its highest court, to undo the decision by attempting to amend its state constitution to ban it. So, the fight continues . . .

Oregon, now a hybrid recognition state—meaning it recognizes out-of-state same-sex marriages, but does not allow them—is perhaps going to undo its ban on same-sex marriage through a ballot initiative. Current polling suggests such a measure would pass. Other states, such as Ohio, Michigan, Pennsylvania, Colorado, Nevada and Utah, may be among the next generation of recognition states to join ranks. This is based on a variety of court cases, and ballot or legislative initiatives that are now underway and likely to come to fruition by 2016. Even Virginia, one of the most hostile states to same-sex couple's legal rights, is under serious watch as rock-star litigators David Boise and Ted Olson (who were on opposite sides of *Bush v. Gore*, but together were successful in the *Perry* case before the Supreme Court in June 2013) work to challenge Virginia's prohibition in court. With recently elected Democratic Governor Terry McAuliffe in support of same-sex marriage, and 56 percent of the population opposing the state's current ban, the path forward seems clear.

But, even with this progress, there are still dozens of states that do not recognize same-sex marriage, and, of course, no federal right to it has yet been determined to exist by the U.S. Supreme Court. So, irrespective of the count (recognition vs. non-recognition states)—the "patchwork" effect of the laws discussed and the principles covered in this book still apply. All of the factors, from a legal, tax and financial planning perspective about whether to wed will always be an issue. In the end, no matter where you live, marriage ultimately comes down to a personal choice that should be made after very careful consideration of a number of critical issues.

For updates on the state of the law and changes among the states, visit:

www.whethertowed.com

# Appendix A:
## State-by-State Analysis of Gay Marriage or other Quasi-Marriage Rights

As previously noted, Massachusetts was the first state to recognize a lawful right for same-sex couples to be married in 2003. Its decision became effective in May of 2004, and since then, it is estimated that more than 22,000 same-sex couples have been married in Massachusetts. It is unclear how many of these are (and remain) residents of Massachusetts, and how many returned home to a different state. In addition, some couples may simply have moved from Massachusetts to other states after being married.

Now, fourteen other states, plus the District of Columbia, currently allow same-sex marriage. On the day of the *Windsor* decision (June 26, 2013), the Pew Research Center published a report suggesting that there were already more than 70,000 same-sex married couples in the United States (likely more), with California (at an estimated 18,000) and New York, at over 12,000, not far behind Massachusetts.*

This appendix will examine where we are on gay marriage state-by-state as of this writing, recognizing that this is not a static thing, and laws and cases change the landscape regularly. I will also identify those hybrid non-recognition states that do not permit same-sex marriages, but that do recognize marriages legalized in other states.

The following is a review of states that have recognition of same-sex marriages (hereinafter "recognition states"); states that have either civil unions or domestic partnership legislation (hereinafter "quasi-marriage states") and states that do not allow or even expressly prohibit same-sex

---

* http://www.pewresearch.org/fact-tank/2013/06/26/how-many-same-sex-marriages-in-the-u-s-at-least-71165-probably-more/

marriages (hereinafter "non-recognition" states). The table at the end is a subset of the last category, hybrid non-recognition states, which are states that don't permit same-sex marriage but recognize some or all of the rights associated with lawfully married same-sex couples who have been married in other states or countries. These are listed in alphabetical order for each category.

## Recognition States

CALIFORNIA: California's history with gay marriage is perhaps the most complex among all of the fifty states.

It began issuing marriage licenses (lawfully)* on June 16, 2008, following the ruling by its state's highest court in the *In re Marriages Cases* decision.[1] There was a strong backlash to this decision that led to a popular ballot initiative commonly referred to as Prop 8—which passed by a narrow margin purporting to amend California's state constitution to allow marriages in California between only one man and one woman.

The constitutionality of that initiative was challenged in Federal District Court and found, by Judge Vaughn Walker to be in violation of the United States Constitution. Judge Walker issued a ruling in that case preventing the governor and secretary of state from implementing Prop 8. That ruling was appealed first to the Ninth Circuit, in which it was upheld, and then appealed to the U.S. Supreme Court in the *Perry v. Hollingsworth* case. The Supreme Court decided the *Perry* case in June 2013 on procedural grounds, effectively clearing the way for gay marriages to resume in California for the first time since 2008. The Court ruled that sponsors of the state's ballot initiative lacked standing to defend it in court. Two days after the Supreme Court decision, the Ninth Circuit Court of Appeals in

---

* In the euphoria of the *Goodridge* decision in Massachusetts in 2003, the mayor of San Francisco ordered the city clerk's office to issue marriage licenses to same-sex couples, and many couples began to marry in California then, too. Those marriages were declared invalid since there was no legal authority to issue those licenses. http://www.nbcnews.com/id/5685429/ns/politics/t/court-annuls-san-francisco-gay-marriages/#.UjSNyMakpCZ

California lifted the stay that prohibited governmental officials from issuing marriage licenses to same-sex couples.

Additionally, as a result of intervening cases and legislation, couples lawfully married after the 2008 case and before the Prop 8 ban were grandfathered in.

Before and in between all this, California did have registered domestic partner legislation on the books that provided all of the same state law rights and benefits to registered domestic partners as same-sex married partners. Since California is a community property state, the effect of all of this remains confusing and will likely be subject to further court cases sorting out the effect of this in, among other areas, tax law for same-sex couples.

CONNECTICUT: In October 2008, Connecticut's Supreme Court ruled that the state's civil union legislation was inadequate from a constitutional perspective, finding that same-sex couples had the same right to civil marriage as their opposite-sex counterparts. Connecticut had enacted a civil union law early in 2005 that became effective October 1, 2005. In April 2010, the state legislature fixed the "mixed bag" status by passing a law that had the effect of converting all previous civil unions to marriage status, and making marriage rights gender neutral, and therefore, available to all couples, effective on October 1, 2010.

DELAWARE: A same-sex marriage bill was passed by the state's legislature and signed into law by its governor in May 2013. Previously, Delaware had civil union legislation on the books since 2012, and the new law allowed conversion from civil union status to marriage when the same-sex marriage law became effective on July 1, 2013. New civil unions are no longer available, and civil unions existing prior to July 1, 2013 must complete conversion by July 1, 2014.

DISTRICT OF COLUMBIA: The D.C. Council approved same-sex marriage in December of 2009; and same-sex marriages began to occur in the District in March 9, 2010. D.C. permits non-residents to come into the District to be married. At that time, Maryland did not allow it; Virginia still does not. Many same-sex couples from those neighboring states did enjoy this access, and came to the District to be married. The effect of those marriages remains to be determined.

In addition, the District was among the first jurisdictions to attempt to recognize registered domestic partnership status since 1992. Since the District's laws are subject to some oversight by Congress, the effect was to block the implementation of this until 2002, when domestic partnership registration became effective in D.C. The District also specifically recognized domestic partnerships and civil union status from other states.

IOWA: The Iowa Supreme Court found a constitutional right to same-sex marriage in a landmark ruling in 2009. Conservative lawmakers attempted to change state law to define marriage as between a man and a woman. Those efforts failed.

MAINE: Maine, like California, has a bit of a complex history. Initially, the Maine Legislature passed a bill allowing same-sex couples to marry, and it was signed into law by the governor on May 6, 2009. Opponents of the bill successfully petitioned for a referendum before the bill became effective and were successful at the ballot box in overturning the legislation in 2009. A subsequent ballot initiative reversed this law when voters approved same-sex marriage in November 2012. Same-sex marriages then began December 29, 2012, thirty days after the vote.

MARYLAND: The legislature first approved domestic partner rights in 2008 (effective July 1, 2008). Same-sex marriage was then passed in February 2012 by the legislature. The issue was then presented to the voters in a ballot initiative that won voter approval in November 2012. This was the first popular vote approval for same-sex marriage in the country. It paved the way for legalization of same-sex marriage effective January 1, 2013. Maryland had, for some time, recognized out-of-state gay marriages, even before it allowed them to take place in-state.

MASSACHUSETTS: Massachusetts was the first state to recognize same-sex marriage. The state's Supreme Judicial Court found that same-sex couples had a constitutional right to marriage under the state's constitution in a landmark ruling in 2003; same-sex marriages began on May 17, 2004.

There was an effort to overturn this decision, led by then Governor Romney, when he convened a series of Constitutional Conventions to amend the Massachusetts Constitution to prohibit same-sex marriages. That effort was successful the first year, 2004, but then failed in 2005. There was another effort in 2006 that was successful, but that one eventually failed in June 2007 securing same-sex marriage rights solidly for that Commonwealth.

MINNESOTA: Voters rejected a constitutional amendment to ban same-sex marriage in 2012. The state legislature followed this by adopting a same-sex marriage bill that was signed into law in May 2013 and took effect August 1, 2013.

NEW HAMPSHIRE: New Hampshire adopted civil union legislation that became effective on January 1, 2008. The legislature approved same-sex marriage in June 2009 and that became effective January 1, 2010. In addition, on January 1, 2011, all civil unions became marriages, unless otherwise dissolved.

NEW JERSEY: New Jersey first adopted domestic partnership legislation in 2004 that provided limited rights in the areas of healthcare, inheritance and property, but not all of the full rights of married couples. In 2006, the New Jersey Supreme Court ruled that unequal dispensation of rights and benefits to committed same-sex partners could not be tolerated under its constitution. The court then ordered the state legislature to fix the problem, which it did by enacting civil union legislation that purported to give same-sex partners all of the same rights, privileges and responsibilities as marriage in 2006. This law was made effective February 19, 2007.

However, a recent (September 27, 2013) decision from a state trial court found that civil unions do not fulfill the court's mandate that gay couples receive equal treatment, in light of the recent Supreme Court decision in *Windsor*. That lower court, therefore, declared that denying same-sex couples the right to equal marriage is unconstitutional and found under the state's equal protection clause that same-sex marriages must now be allowed in New Jersey. The state's highest court, however, denied a motion to "stay" the lower court decision pending appeal finding that continuing to deny this right to same-couples would cause irreparable harm, and that the appeal was unlikely to be successful in a decision dated October 18, 2013. Therefore, state officials were allowed to issue marriages licenses to otherwise eligible same-sex couples beginning on October 21, 2013.[2] Governor Chris Christie announced the following day he would drop the appeal of the case, thus ensuring marriage licenses would remain available in New Jersey.

NEW YORK: This state also has a checkered past.* New York's highest court ruled in 2006 that its state constitution did not "require" same-sex marriage rights and left the issue to the legislature. Following this decision, the New York State Assembly passed a bill authorizing same-sex marriage in 2007, 2009 and 2011, but the Senate failed to pass the law in the early years. Finally, in 2011, both houses of the state's legislature approved same-sex marriage on June 24, 2011, effective July 24, 2011.

RHODE ISLAND: A same-sex marriage bill was signed into law in May 2013 that took effect August 1, 2013. This state had recognized unregistered domestic partners since 2002 and passed civil union legislation in 2011, effective July 1, 2011. This bill, however, included controversial provisions that allowed any religiously affiliated institutions, such as schools, hospitals and universities, to deny recognition of civil unions.

Recognition of out-of-state same-sex marriages had a confusing history here, too. In February 2007, the state's attorney general issued an opinion stating that Rhode Island should recognize same-sex marriages from Massachusetts. However, in December of 2007, the state's highest court ruled that its courts did not have jurisdiction over a divorce from a same-sex marriage from Massachusetts.

VERMONT: Same-sex marriage began on September 1, 2009, by virtue of legislative action (which overrode a governor's veto—the first time for Vermont in nearly twenty years). With this, Vermont became the first state to authorize same-sex marriage by statute, and not by virtue of a court decision.

Prior to this, Vermont's highest state court was the first to announce that same-sex couples were entitled to some form of legal recognition in 1999, stopping short of requiring marriage. Its state legislature responded to that decision by adopting the first civil union legislation in the country, recognizing gay and lesbian couples right to all the same benefits as marriage for all state law purposes. That legislation was signed into law by then-Governor Howard Dean and became effective on July 1, 2000.

---

* Similar to the San Francisco mayor, New York's New Paltz Mayor Jason West married twenty-five same-sex couples in February 2004 without legal authority. Nineteen misdemeanor counts were brought against this mayor by prosecutors, but they were eventually dropped.

WASHINGTON: The Legislature approved same-sex marriage in February 2012. Implementation of the law was blocked by a ballot initiative that failed. Same-sex marriage won voter approval in referendum on November 6, 2012, becoming effective on Dec 6, 2010. Marriages began on December 9, 2012.

*Andersen v. King County*, 138 P.3d 963 (Wash. 2006) is a case in which eight same-sex couples sued King County and the state of Washington for denying them marriage licenses under the state's 1998 Defense of Marriage Act (mini-DOMA), which defined marriage as between a man and a woman. The Washington Supreme Court ruled in that case that banning same-sex marriage was constitutional.

NATIVE AMERICAN TRIBAL JURISDICTIONS: While we have not conducted an extensive search of laws in this area, it is reported that at least five Native American Tribes recognize same-sex marriages for their respective jurisdictions. These include: Coquille Tribe (Oregon) 2008; Suquarnish Tribe (Washington) 2011; Little Traverse Bay Bands of Odawa Indians (Michigan) 2013; Pokagon Band Potawatomi Indians (Michigan) 2013; and Santa Ysabel Tribe (California) 2013.[3]

# Quasi-Recognition States (Domestic Partner and Civil Union)

This is the most confusing category, and will be subject to change, no doubt, as soon as the ink is dry in this book. Many states afford same-sex couples certain (sometimes full) rights and benefits under special legislation commonly referred to as civil unions and/or domestic partnerships. In those same states, some of them specifically prohibit recognition of same-sex marriage by that state, BUT do recognize other states' same-sex marriages (e.g. Illinois), and is therefore a quasi-recognition state. Other states recognize some form of legal right for same-sex couples, but specifically prohibit recognition of same-sex marriage from another state (a non-recognition state). Still others offer no form of in-state recognition, nor do they allow or recognize same-sex marriages from others states. The full non-recognition list is below.

The list here includes all states with some form of legal recognition of a same-sex relationship that is short of marriage—meaning either civil unions or domestic partnerships. Where evident, we have also addressed the "recognition/non-recognition" question. Given the pending cases in many of these states, couples are advised to consult with a local lawyer for the current status, and not rely entirely on this summary.

COLORADO: Civil unions have been lawful and recognized since May 1, 2013. This provides same-sex couples with comparable rights and privileges as married couples in the state for state law purposes. However, by ballot initiative, Colorado voters amended its state constitution by banning recognition of same-sex marriage (including common law marriages) in November 2006.

As far back as 1975, however, authorities in Colorado were debating this question. The Boulder county clerk issued marriage licenses to same-sex couples based on a district attorney's opinion that Colorado statutes referring to "any two persons" is gender neutral. The state's attorney general disagreed and issued his own opinion that those marriages were invalid. One couple married during this time attempted to use that marriage as justification for one man to sponsor his male spouse for federal immigration purposes. That petition was denied in federal court.[4]

HAWAII: Some scholars believe it all started here. And, those in the know think Hawaii may become the next recognition state. In 1993, Hawaii's highest state court ruled that the failure to grant same-sex couples marriage licenses was unlawful and discriminatory under the state's constitution. In 1998, voters adopted a constitutional amendment reserving for the legislature the power to restrict marriage to only opposite-sex couples, which it later did by passing a "mini-DOMA" type law later that same year.

Lawmakers later passed a civil union law in 2011, and the state began to implement civil unions on January 1, 2012. There is a bill currently pending before the state's legislature which would allow same-sex marriage.

Similar to some other cases, a same-sex couple from Hawaii has brought a case in federal court claiming the denial of their right to marry in Hawaii violated the U.S. Constitution.

ILLINOIS: Lawmakers approved civil unions, giving same-sex couples virtually the same benefits of marriage for state law purposes when that law became effective June 1, 2011. In 1996, the legislature had adopted, effectively, a mini-DOMA type statute to prohibit marriage between same-sex couples; some believe this was in reaction to the Hawaii Supreme Court case. Illinois also has a same-sex marriage bill pending. There are also cases pending in state court challenging the state's refusal to grant same-sex marriage licenses.

NEVADA: Since 2002, Nevada has been among those states that have a constitutional ban on same-sex marriage, but it also has a domestic partnership law that has been in effect since October 1, 2009. The law provides the same rights to same-sex couples as opposite-sex married couples. Legislators approved a resolution in 2013 aimed at repealing the constitutional ban on allowing same-sex marriage; it will need a second round of legislative approval in two years before going to a popular vote in 2016. Meanwhile, there is a case pending in the Ninth Circuit Court challenging the constitutionality of the ban.

OREGON: Domestic partnership legislation was signed into law in May 2007 that provided virtually all of the same rights and benefits of married couples to same-sex couples choosing to register as domestic partners. Following the law's passage, there were several court challenges, all of which were unsuccessful. The domestic partner law became effective February 1, 2008. Subsequent to this, the law was amended to specifically recognize domestic partners and civil unions from other states.

However, in a November 2004 ballot initiative, voters in Oregon approved a constitutional amendment that effectively banned same-sex marriage in this state—another mini-DOMA. This constitutional amendment has the potential to be undone by another ballot initiative in 2014.

Although same-sex marriages are not performed in Oregon, the state does now recognize same-sex marriages performed elsewhere, as a result of an October 16, 2013 legal opinion from Oregon Deputy Attorney General Mary Williams.[5]

WISCONSIN: By a 2006 ballot initiative, voters adopted a "mini-DOMA," which has had the effect of banning same-sex marriage in the state, as well as blocking any other condition identical or similar to marriage.

This has had the effect of also banning full civil union and/or domestic partner legislation.

Notwithstanding this, in 2009, the legislature passed a law creating a limited domestic partner registry for same-sex couples. This registry includes some forty-three rights (out of over 200) that mostly deal with inheritance, and health and property issues. At least one state court ruled this law does not violate the state's constitutional ban, and that ruling has been affirmed on appeal.

## Non-Recognition States

ALABAMA: Voters approved a constitutional amendment in 2006 banning recognition of same-sex marriages and civil unions by an over-whelming majority of the population.

ALASKA: Voters approved a ban of same-sex marriage in 1998 by amending their constitution to define marriage as being between one man and one woman (mini-DOMA). Interestingly, however, Alaska's state employees have some limited benefits for same-sex domestic partners. In addition, many cities in Alaska have passed local ordinances granting rights to same-sex partners.

ARIZONA: In 2008, voters adopted a constitutional amendment to ban gay marriage. The state also does not recognize civil unions or domestic partnerships, although some municipalities do, such as Bisbee and Tucson. Other municipalities are considering similar ordinances. Although a 2014 ballot measure to overturn the prior constitutional ban was contemplated, Arizona residents will not be asked to vote on the issue in 2014.

ARKANSAS: Although this state's highest court found that criminal laws outlawing sex between people of the same gender violated the state's constitution, voters banned recognition of both same-sex marriage and civil unions in 2004. Following the recent U.S. Supreme Court decision in *Windsor,* concerned citizens filed both a ballot initiative to undo the state's constitutional ban, and have filed lawsuits alleging the current ban violates the state's constitutional guarantees of due process, equal protection and of privacy. They further allege the state's ban violates the federal constitutional provision of full faith and credit. Eureka Springs in Carroll County is the only known municipality in the state to recognize domestic partnership rights by ordinance. It has provided healthcare coverage for same-sex domestic partners since 2011.

FLORIDA: Voters amended the state constitution in November 2008, banning same-sex marriages and civil unions. A variety of counties and cities in Florida, however, offer domestic partner benefits to its employees in same-gender relationships.

GEORGIA: Voters passed a constitutional amendment in 2004 banning gay marriage. Some municipalities maintain a domestic partner registry for its employees in same-sex relationships for purposes of offering certain benefits.

IDAHO: Voters banned same-sex marriage by amending its constitution in 2006.

INDIANA: There is a state law prohibiting same-sex marriage, but, as yet, no constitutional ban. A ban has been proposed, however, and will be put to a legislative vote early in 2014. Leaders of the Republican majority in the legislature hope the Supreme Court rulings will provide motivation to get the ban passed so it can be put before voters in 2014. GOP Governor Mike Pence says he supports a stronger ban. Not only are gay marriages banned in the state, but anyone who officiates at a ceremony solemnizing a same-sex union can be fined or incarcerated. As of July 1, 2014, same-sex couples who even apply for a marriage license in the state will have committed a felony and could face jail time.

KANSAS: Voters passed a gay-marriage ban in 2005. State statutes also ban recognition of same-gender relationships for a variety of purposes. Lawrence is the only municipality in the state to offer same-sex partner benefits by local ordinance.

KENTUCKY: Voters approved a ban on same-sex marriage in 2004. While there are similar prohibitions in certain state statutes, one statute does provide recognition for same-sex couples' rights for hospital visitation.

Kentucky happened to be the site of one of the very first court challenges around gay marriage in 1973, where a lesbian couple's claim was essentially summarily dismissed.

LOUISIANA: Voters banned same-sex marriage and civil unions (but not domestic partnerships) by amending its constitution in 2004. The state's civil code (since 1999) also specifically prohibits recognition of same-sex marriages from other states.

MICHIGAN: Voters amended its constitution in 2004, banning same-sex marriage and civil unions. Based on this provision, this state's highest court went on to rule that most public employers were banned from extending health and other benefits to employees in same-sex couple relationships. That ban was challenged in federal district court, and in 2013 a federal judge issued an injunction to stop the state from this ban of health benefits to domestic partners. That case is still pending, in part, as a result of the Supreme Court's ruling in *Windsor.* Separately, citizen activists are attempting to get a measure on the ballot in 2016 to overturn the constitutional ban.

MISSISSIPPI: This state wins the prize for one of the most restrictive sets of laws against same-sex couples (tied, perhaps with Virginia). Both by state statute and by constitutional amendment (passed in 2004), the state has banned same-sex marriages and any form of same-sex partnerships solemnized in any other jurisdiction.

MISSOURI: This state's voters amended its constitution in 2004 to ban same-sex marriages. The state also does not recognize marriages from other states, even if valid where performed. The state Supreme Court is considering a legal challenge to a law that limits survivor benefits for deceased public safety officers to spouses who were in a "marriage between a man and a woman." The case was brought by the same-sex (but unmarried) partner of a former highway patrol officer struck and killed by a vehicle on Christmas Day 2009 while investigating an accident.

MONTANA: Voters amended its constitution to ban same-sex marriages in 2004. That same year, this state's highest court found, however, that state universities' policy of denying same-sex partner health benefits violated the state constitutional equal protection requirements. Since 2005, Montana has provided same-sex partner benefits to its state employees. There are other cases pending that challenge state statutes that deny rights to same-sex couples.

NEBRASKA: Voters passed a constitutional amendment to prohibit recognition of same-sex marriage, or any other rights of same-sex couples (however named), in 2000. That law was successfully challenged in federal district court, but overturned on appeal (and review was not sought by the U.S. Supreme Court in that case.) The state did pass a designated visitor statute to extend hospital visitation rights to same-sex couples.

NEW MEXICO: Its statutes contain no law that specifically prohibits or legalizes same-sex marriage. Nor is it clear whether the state would recognize same-sex marriages issued in other states. It is the only state in which its position on same-sex marriage is so unclear. Democratic Attorney General Gary King's office released a legal analysis in early June concluding that same-sex marriage is not authorized at this point. But lawyers for two gay men from Santa Fe are trying to expedite a lawsuit seeking a ruling that gay marriage is legal. There are currently several lawsuits pending.

NORTH CAROLINA: Late to the "banning" game, voters in North Carolina amended its constitution in May 2012 banning recognition of same-sex marriage and all other forms of same-sex unions. Its state statutes also ban recognition of same-sex marriages and all other types of same-sex unions. The state does have a designated visitor statute to extend hospital visitation rights to same-sex couples. Some towns have recognized domestic partners by virtue of registration, and others have offered same-sex partner benefits to employees of its municipalities.

NORTH DAKOTA: Voters amended its constitution to ban same-sex marriage and prohibit recognition of civil unions and domestic partnerships in 2004. Its state legislature has repeatedly voted against gay-rights measures, including a bill to prohibit discrimination based on sexual orientation in housing, public services and the workplace.

OHIO: A constitutional amendment banning same-sex marriages and civil unions was approved in November 2004, but it did not affect domestic partner registries. Citizen activists are attempting to undo this in either 2014 or 2016.

Certain cities in Ohio provide domestic partnership registries locally.

OKLAHOMA: Same-sex marriages and other forms of same-sex partnerships solemnized in other jurisdictions were banned both by statute and constitutional amendment in 2004.

PENNSYLVANIA: Since 1996, there has been a statutory ban on same-sex marriages, with marriage defined as one man and one woman. Pennsylvania is the only state in the Northeast that doesn't extend legal recognition to same-sex couples. An openly gay Democratic State Representative Brian Sims plans to introduce a bill that would legalize same-sex marriage. It may not get far in the GOP-controlled legislature, but it could be an issue in the 2014 gubernatorial campaign. Incumbent GOP Governor Tom Corbett opposes gay marriage; the three Democratic challengers support it. On July 24, 2013, the Montgomery County register of wills announced he would issue marriage licenses to same-sex couples based on his reading of the state constitution, but then was sued by the Pennsylvania Department of Health on July 30, 2013, for violating state law.

SOUTH CAROLINA: In 2006, voters amended its constitution to define marriage as being between "one man and one woman," effectively banning same-sex marriage and prohibiting recognition of same-sex relationships by any other name. Similar restrictions are in its state statutes.

SOUTH DAKOTA: Same-sex marriage was prohibited by this state's legislature in 1996. The voters later amended its constitution to ban same-sex marriages and to prohibit recognition by any other name, such as civil union and domestic partnership in 2006.

TENNESSEE: Voters amended its state constitution to ban same-sex marriages in 2006, and further prohibits, by statute, recognition of same-sex relationships solemnized in other jurisdictions.

TEXAS: In 1997, the state legislature prohibited issuance of marriage licenses to same-sex couples, by statute. Later, in 2003, the legislature enacted a statute to void any same-sex marriage or civil union for state law purposes performed anywhere. There has been debate about whether this law violates the federal full faith and credit clause of the U.S. Constitution.

Voters amended its state constitution in 2005 to define a marriage by one man and one woman (mini-DOMA) and to prohibit the state or any political subdivision of the state from creating or recognizing any legal status identical, or similar, to marriage. A federal lawsuit is pending challenging this.

Some municipalities have, nonetheless, offered domestic partner benefits to their employees, much to the chagrin of the state's attorney general. Disputes abound.

UTAH: Three same-sex couples have filed a legal challenge against Utah's gay-marriage ban, which was approved by voters in 2004. The case had been put on hold pending the U.S. Supreme Court rulings. Utah's 1995 "Recognition of Marriages" bill was the first law to ever prohibit state recognition of same-sex marriages performed outside the state. A 2010 Columbia University opinion poll found that Utah ranked last among all states in its support of same-sex marriage.

VIRGINIA: Two same-sex couples in the state filed a second class-action suit in August 2013 challenging Virginia's restrictive marriage laws. Voters approved a ban in 2006. It's unlikely that the legislature, which is dominated by conservative Republicans, would take steps to repeal the ban. Gay-rights supporters haven't ruled out a lawsuit. The Marshall-Newman Amendment expressly prohibits the state, and any of its municipalities, from recognizing any form of relationship, such as domestic partnerships or civil unions, between same-sex partners. Virginia is one of only fifteen states with hate crime laws that do not include crimes based on sexual orientation or gender identity.

WEST VIRGINA: Under a state law passed in 2000, West Virginia defines marriage as being between a man and a woman. The state does not have a constitutional ban, though some Republicans in the legislature say they will intensify their push for one because of the Supreme Court rulings. A December 2011 bill introduced to legalize civil unions in the state was also shot down.

WYOMING: Despite being called the "equality state," Wyoming law defines marriage as a civil contract between a man and a woman; there is no constitutional ban. Democratic State Representative Cathy Connolly, a lesbian, pushed legislation earlier this year that would have permitted civil unions and banned discrimination against gays. Both bills died. She expects a proposal for legalizing gay marriage to be introduced by 2015; there's also the possibility of a lawsuit seeking marriage equality.

TABLE A.1 HYBRID NON-RECOGNITION STATES

| State | Status |
|---|---|
| Oregon | The state's Attorney General has issued an opinion stating that all state agencies should recognizes otherwise valid same-sex marriages performed elsewhere, but does not allow them. |
| New Mexico | The state has no ban on same-sex marriage, but it also does not outright approve it. Some counties have begun issuing marriage licenses to same-sex couples and there is litigation pending to resolve it. |
| Ohio | The state is currently subject to a Temporary Restraining Order that does not allow it to enforce its ban on same-sex marriage for certain purposes, notably for issuing death certificates for married persons elsewhere. |
| Illinois | The broad "Illinois Religious Freedom Protection and Civil Union Act" came into effect in 2011. Section 60 of that act provides that, "A marriage between persons of the same sex, a civil union, or a substantially similar legal relationship other than common law marriage, legally entered into in another jurisdiction, shall be recognized in Illinois as a civil union." |
| Oklahoma | Residents of the state of Oklahoma are permitted to be married on tribal lands that recognize same-sex unions. Those marriages, however, will not be recognized by the state. |

## Overview of Recognition by Other Countries

Argentina, Belgium, Brazil, Canada, Denmark, France, Iceland, Netherlands, New Zealand, Norway, Portugal, South Africa, Spain, Sweden, and Uruguay all now recognize same-sex marriage.

Mexico City and the Mexican state of Quintana Roo also recognize same-sex marriage.

Other jurisdictions recognize same-sex marriages from other jurisdictions, but don't perform or allow these marriages to be solemnized in their jurisdiction: Aruba, Curacao, St. Maarten, Israel and Mexico (if performed somewhere in Mexico where lawful)

In addition, the following foreign jurisdictions recognize from a legal perspective some form of rights for gay couples (short of marriage) in the form of civil unions or domestic partnerships:

Andorra, Austria, Columbia, Czech Republic, Ecuador, Finland, Germany, Greenland, Hungary, Ireland, Isle of Man, Jersey, Liechtenstein, Luxembourg, Slovenia , Switzerland, United Kingdom, and some limited jurisdictions within the following countries: Austria, Mexico, Venezuela.

# Appendix B:
## Web Resources

List of online resources:

1. Whether to Wed, www.whethertowed.com
2. Gay Estate Planning, www.gayestateplanning.com
3. GLAD, www.glad.org
4. Human Rights Campaign, www.hrc.org
5. ACLU, www.aclu.org/lgbt-rights
6. Freedom to Marry, www.freedomtomarry.org
7. Tax Equity Project, www.lgbtbar.org/tax-equity-project
8. Family Equality Council, www.familyequality.org
9. Lambda Legal, www.lambdalegal.org
10. National Center for Lesbian Rights, www.nclrights.org
11. Lesbian and Gay Law Notes, www.nyls.edu/centers/ harlan_scholar_centers/justice_action_center/publications/ lesbiangay_law_notes
12. The Williams Institute at UCLA, www.williamsinstitute.law. ucla.edu

# Appendix C:
## Glossary

**Affordable Care Act**—Known more commonly as "Obama-care," this new federally-mandated health care program was designed to increase the quality and affordability of health insurance while also increasing the number of insured Americans nationwide.

**Alternative minimum tax**—A nearly flat income tax applied to taxable income above a certain maximum amount that is higher than the ordinary income tax exemption amount. It has the effect of limiting or sometimes eliminating the availability of certain deductions.

**Artificial Reproductive Technology or Alternative Reproductive Therapies (both, short-handed as "ART")**—Forms of reproduction, such as in vitro fertilization or artificial insemination, that can enable couples to become pregnant without sexual intercourse.

**Beneficiary designation forms**—Forms related to life insurance, retirement plans or annuities that specify who should receive certain payouts at death. They are often governed by the underlying plan documents and sometimes by law.

**Bi-national couple**—Two people in a relationship who are nationals of (meaning, they hold passports from) two different countries.

**Buy-sell agreement**—Sometimes called a business will, or a shareholders' agreement, this type of agreement, signed by owners of a business, defines what happens to the owner's interest in the company if one dies, or leaves the active management of the firm, or if an owner divorces or needs to file for bankruptcy protection. It's like a prenuptial agreement for business owners.

**Child tax credit**—A federal income tax credit of $1,000 per child given to families earning less than $110,000 a year; above that, the credit is phased out. If income is significantly below $110,000, a larger credit may be given.

**Civil union**—A form of relationship created to acknowledge same-sex couples without calling it "marriage." Couples in formal civil unions, which are registered, are granted many of the same rights, benefits, and obligations as married couples, but on a state level. But civil unions are not recognized by the federal government for marriage rights.

**Community property state**—A U.S. state, such as California, Oregon or Washington, that grants spouses a one-half interest in the other spouse's income and assets acquired during the marriage. This has certain tax consequences and affects divorces differently in these states.

**Consolidated Omnibus Budget Reconciliation Act (COBRA)**—A federal law that guarantees newly-unemployed workers be offered continued insurance coverage for up to eighteen months after being fired or let go with certain requirements, usually including that the terminated employee must pay the employer's cost of the health insurance to continue it.

**Coverture**—An antiquated legal concept whereby the wife's legal interest was merged into the husband's to become one legal entity.

**Death tax**—Also referred to as estate tax, and is the amount taxed on an estate. It can be applied by the federal government and in some states, by the state. As of January 1, 2013, the highest marginal tax rate federally is 40 percent, which is applied to the total value of an estate over $5.25 million/person, or $10.5 million for all married couples. These numbers could change each year, since they are indexed for inflation.

**DOMA**—Defense of Marriage Act. A U.S. federal law enacted in 1996 that allowed states to refuse to recognize same-sex marriages performed in other states, and allowed the federal government to not recognize any same-sex marriage for federal law purposes.

**Domestic partnership**—A legal form of relationship that, in some states, is almost the equivalent of marriage in terms of the rights and benefits conferred and, in other states, provides fewer rights for unmarried couples, sometimes not even in an intimate relationship, and can be akin to co-habitation rights.

**Due-on-sale clause**—A clause in most mortgages that requires the balance of the mortgage to be paid in full if there is any changes made to the owners listed on the deed, indicating a sale. However, a federal law called Garn St. Germain disallows such actions when the reason the deed is changed is for marriage, now including same-sex marriage.

**Employment Retirement Income Security Act (ERISA)**—The federal law governing retirement and similar pension and qualified plans provided by employers.

**Family and Medical Leave Act (FMLA)**—A federal law that requires that employers with fifty or more employees must grant employees up to twelve weeks of unpaid leave per year to care for newborn children, to care for a spouse or immediate family member, or to recover from a serious medical illness.

**Family attribution rules**—Regulations promulgated by the IRS to close certain wealth transfer loopholes within families without tax consequences.

**Fourteenth Amendment**—This amendment grants "equal protection under the law," which is a key point in the same-sex marriage fight. Treating same-sex couples as different is counter to this amendment, many contend. It applies to all actions of state and local officials, but not private citizens.

**GLAD**—An acronym for Gay and Lesbian Advocates and Defenders, a New England-based non-profit organization dedicated to advocating for the rights of LBGTQ Americans and fighting for equality.

**Healthcare proxy**—A legal document signed by an individual designating who should make medical decisions in their place, should they be unable to make such decisions for themselves.

**Hybrid non-recognition states**—This refers to states that do not allow same-sex marriage in their state, but recognize for some or all purposes same-sex marriages lawfully performed in other states or foreign countries.

**IRA spousal rollover**—The opportunity to take all the money in one IRA upon the death of the account holder and roll it over, meaning transfer it, into a new IRA, generally without penalty, in order to continue tax-deferred compounding. This is only available for spouses.

**IRA stretch-out**—The opportunity upon death of the account holder for beneficiaries (other than a spouse) to defer taking inherited IRA money out all at once and paying the income tax due and instead, "stretch" it out for the new beneficiary's lifetime. It is a one-time election that must be made by September 15 of the year following the year of the death that caused the IRA to be inherited. It is subject to special IRS rules.

**Joint-ownership agreement**—Agreements that outline all of the provisions that need to be considered if certain events occur, such as divorce or death. Such agreements can include buy-sell provisions that outline who gets what and for how much if the couple splits up.

**Joint tenants with rights of survivorship (JTWRS)**—A form of ownership designed to ensure the joint owner inherits a co-owned property. It is a common way for unmarried couples to title property.

**LGBTQ**—An acronym for the lesbian, bisexual and transgender community. Sometimes a Q is added to represent those who identify as "queer" or may be questioning their sexual identity.

**Long-term care insurance (LTC)**—Insurance purchased to help cover the cost of continued medical care, such as in a nursing home or assisted living setting. It can also cover certain in-home expenses for aging people who want to remain at home but need care as they age.

**Marriage bonus**—A personal income tax situation that can arise when one spouse earns considerably more than the other, such as when one is a stay-at-home parent. By combining both salaries, the marginal tax rate often declines by comparison to what each individual paid as a single filer.

**Marriage equality movement**—the political, legal and social efforts made by gay and lesbians and their allies to obtain equal access to the right of civil marriage.

**Marriage penalty**—A personal income tax situation that can arise when both spouses earn similar amounts. Once married, the joint tax rate may be higher than the tax rate applied to each spouse individually.

**Married filing jointly (MFJ)**—A tax filing status available only to legally married couples.

**Married filing separately (MFS)**—A tax filing status that allows married couples to elect to file two separate income tax returns. This option is usually worse for total income tax payments, but may be used when one spouse does not want to participate in another spouse's risky tax schemes.

**Medicaid**—The federal health benefit program administered by the states for lower income citizens that provides healthcare coverage when the individual or family cannot afford it. There are limits to the value of the assets the individual or family can have and still qualify.

**Medicare**—The federal health insurance program designed to assist with the costs of health care for Americans over age sixty-five. Part A covers hospital stays, nursing facilities, and hospice care, while Part B covers medical insurance, outpatient care, doctors' services, and preventive care. Part C is a private health plan, and Part D includes prescription drug coverage.

**Non-recognition state**—A state that does not permit same-sex marriages. (It is important to note that some of these states may recognize out-of-state same-sex marriages, even though they do not permit or recognize the right of same-sex couples to be married in their state. Those states are a sub-set of this group and referred to herein as hybrid non-recognition states.)

**Prenuptial agreement**—An agreement drafted and signed prior to a valid marriage being solemnized that outlines who gets what in the event of a divorce, and other issues regarding property rights and, sometimes, inheritance rights. Often used when one party has significantly more assets going into the marriage than the other.

**Proxy marriage**—A marriage ceremony where someone else stands in for one of the individuals being married. The ability to not be present at your own wedding started as a way for military personnel deployed overseas to be married when they couldn't be at the ceremony in person.

**Recognition state**—A state that recognizes the right of same-sex couples to be married in that sate and therefore recognizes all attendant rights, privileges and obligations that go with marriage, irrespective of the couple's gender.

**Required Minimum Distribution (RMD)**—The amount you must draw from your retirement account each year, based on your age, currently required to begin by age seventy-and-a-half.

**Revocable Living Trust (RLT)**—A type of trust that can be changed by the trust maker at any point during their life, but that specifies who receives their assets upon their death.

**SCOTUS**—An acronym for the Supreme Court of The United States.

**Second-parent adoption**—The practice of a non-biological parent to legally adopt their same-sex spouse's child(ren).

**Split-gifting**—The opportunity that married couples have to combine the annual gift exclusion (currently at $14,000 per person, per year) to give someone double that amount (currently $28,000), irrespective of who in a married couple funds the gift.

**Spousal elective share right**—Governed by state law, this provides an option to a surviving spouse to accept (generally) one-half of everything in the estate—called "electing against the will"—instead of what the spouse left in his or her will or trust. This law effectively guarantees that at least half of any married person's estate will go to his or her spouse.

**Supplemental Security Income (SSI)**—A Social Security benefit for low-income people who are over age sixty-five, or are blind or disabled.

**Tenancy in common (TIC)**—A form of holding title to property that allows two or more people to own an undivided percentage interest with no rights of survivorship. That means at death, one spouse's ownership could be transferred to children or another party other than the spouse.

**Tenants by the entirety (T by E)**—The typical way married couples hold title to real estate, which is available only to married couples in recognition states, or states that recognize out-of-state marriages. In this case, the surviving spouse automatically inherits the other's interest in the property at death and provides protection against creditors should a lawsuit arise that threatens ownership of the property.

**Trust**—A type of contract where property or assets are held by a trustee for the benefit of someone else, known as the beneficiar(ies). There are many types of trusts, but generally they are either revocable (meaning changeable) or irrevocable.

**Unlimited marital deduction**—The law that allows any U.S. citizen spouse (same or opposite-sex) to leave another U.S. citizen spouse any amount of money and not be subject to federal estate taxes, or state estate taxes (if living in a recognition state).

# Appendix D:
## Relationship Recognition Timeline

Marriage States*:

### *Massachusetts:*
440 Mass. 309 (2003)

**Goodridge v. Dept. of Public Health decision legalizing marriage:** November 18, 2003

**Marriage licenses issued:** May 17, 2004

### *California (part 1):*

**Limited domestic partnership law enacted:** October 2, 1999

**Domestic partnerships performed:** January 1, 2000

**Domestic partnership rights become identical to marriage:** January 1, 2005

1. The law applied retroactively to all Registered Domestic Partnerships (RDPs, or DPs) that were not terminated prior to the statute's effective date of January 1, 2005.

2. The means of establishing or dissolving a DP are different than marriage.

**Couples in domestic partnerships must file a joint state tax return, like married couples:** effective in 2007 tax year

---

* Listed chronologically by date marriage licenses issued.

*In re Marriage Cases* **legalizes marriage:** May 15, 2008

**Marriage licenses issued:** June 17, 2008

**Marriages stop being performed when Prop. 8 referendum passes:** November 4, 2008

### Connecticut:
2009 Conn. Pub. Acts no. 09–13

**Civil unions law enacted:** April 20, 2005

**Civil unions performed:** October 1, 2005

*Kerrigan* **decision legalizing marriage:** October 10, 2008

**Marriage licenses issued:** November 12, 2008

**All remaining civil unions converted to marriage:** October 1, 2010

### Iowa:
763 N. W. 2d 862 (Iowa 2009)

*Varnum v. Brien* **decision legalizing marriage:** April 3, 2009

**Marriage licenses issued:** April 27, 2009

### Vermont:
Vt. Stat. Ann., Tit. 15, §8

*Baker v. Vermont* **decision finding a constitutional violation but not offering a remedy:** December 20, 1999

**Civil unions law enacted:** April 26, 2000

**Civil unions performed:** July 1, 2000

**Marriage law enacted (over governor's veto):** April 7, 2009

**Marriage licenses issued:** September 1, 2009

**Civil unions no longer performed:** September 1, 2009. Couples who entered into civil unions between July 1, 2000 and September 1, 2009 will still have their unions recognized. If these couples wish to get married, they may do so by obtaining a marriage license.

## New Hampshire:
### N. H. Rev. Stat. Ann. §457:1–a

**Civil unions law enacted:** June 4, 2007

**Civil unions performed:** January 1, 2008

**Marriage law enacted:** June 3, 2009

**Marriage licenses issued:** January 1, 2010

**Civil unions no longer performed:** January 1, 2010

**All remaining civil unions converted to marriage:** January 1, 2011

## District of Columbia:
### 57 D. C. Reg. 27

**Very limited domestic partnership law takes effect:** June 14, 2002 (applies only to certain healthcare benefits)

**Marriage law enacted:** December 18, 2009

**Marriage licenses issued:** March 3, 2010 (licenses available); March 9, 2010 (marriages performed)

**Status of domestic partnerships:** Same-sex and different-sex couples can still opt to get a domestic partnership in D.C., rather than get married.

## New York:
### N. Y. Dom. Rel. Law Ann. §10–a

***Hernandez v. Robles* decision—no constitutional right to same-sex marriage:** July 1, 2006

**Marriage law enacted:** June 24, 2011

**Marriage licenses issued:** July 24, 2011

## *Washington:*
### RCW 26.04.010

**Limited domestic partnership law enacted:** April 21, 2007 (hospital visitation, participation in medical care decision-making, access to healthcare information, estate administration, recognition of partner on death certificate, ability to sue for wrongful death of a partner, right to inherit property and to administer the partner's estate in absence of a will.)

**Domestic partnerships performed:** July 22, 2007

**Expanded domestic partnership protections:** 2008 (expanded rights, including dissolutions, community property, estate planning, taxes, court processes, service to indigent veterans and other public assistance, conflicts of interest for public officials, guardianships)

**Domestic partnerships with rights identical to marriage:** December 3, 2009

**Marriage referendum:** November 6, 2012

**Marriage licenses issued:** December 9, 2012

**Status of domestic partnerships (DP):** All DPs where at least one partner is *NOT* age sixty-two or over on June 30, 2014 will automatically be converted to marriages on June 30, 2014. If at least one partner is sixty-two-plus, they will remain in a DP unless, and until, they choose to get married.

## *Maine:*
### 19-A M.R.S. § 650-A

**Limited domestic partnership law enacted:** April 28, 2004 (matters of probate, guardianships, conservatorships, inheritance, protection from abuse, some health matters)

**Domestic partnerships performed:** July 30, 2004

**Marriage law enacted:** May 6, 2009

**2009 voter referendum overturning marriage law:** November 3, 2009

**2012 voter referendum legalizing marriage:** November 6, 2012

**Marriage licenses issued:** December 29, 2012

## *Maryland:*
Md. Fam. Law Code Ann. §2–201

**Very limited domestic partnership law enacted:** May 22, 2008 (only pertains to hospital visitation and other medical decision-making and to joint property ownership)

**Domestic partnerships performed:** July 1, 2008

**Marriage referendum:** November 6, 2012

**Marriage licenses issued:** January 1, 2013 (though licenses could begin being issued on December 6, 2012, so long as the effective date specified January 1, 2013)

**Status of domestic partnerships (DP):** The two DP statutes were not repealed by the law granting marriages to same-sex couples. Qualified couples (both same-sex and different-sex) still appear to be able to enter into a domestic partnership.

## *California (part 2):*

**After the U.S. Supreme Court decided *Perry v. Hollingsworth*, marriage licenses issued again:** June 28, 2013.

## *Delaware:*
79 Del. Laws ch. 19

**Civil unions law enacted:** May 11, 2011

**Civil unions performed:** January 1, 2012

**Marriage law enacted:** May 7, 2013

**Marriage licenses issued:** July 1, 2013

**Status of civil unions:** On July 1, 2014, all remaining civil unions not in the process of dissolution will be automatically converted to marriages.

## *Rhode Island:*
2013 R. I. Laws ch. 4.

**Civil unions law enacted:** July 2, 2011

**Civil unions performed:** July 1, 2011 (retroactively took effect)

**Marriage law enacted:** May 2, 2013

**Marriage licenses issued:** August 1, 2013

**Status of civil unions:** Civil unions will stop being performed on August 1, 2013. Couples who entered into civil unions between July 1, 2011 and July 31, 2013 will still have their unions recognized. If these couples wish to get married, they may do so by obtaining a marriage license.

## *Minnesota:*
2013 Minn. Laws ch. 74

**Marriage law passed:** May 13, 2013

**Marriags law signed by governor:** May 14, 2013

**Marriage licenses issued:** August 1, 2013

## *New Jersey:*

***Lewis v. Harris* decision finding it unconstitutional to deny same-sex couples equal rights and responsibilities in their relationships:** October 25, 2006

**Civil unions law enacted:** December 21, 2006

**Civil unions performed:** February 19, 2007

***Garden State Equality v. Paula Dow et. al.* decision finding constitutional right to marry. September 27, 2013, NJ S. Ct. ruled October 18, 2013**

**Marriage licenses issued:** October 21, 2013

# Civil Union/Domestic Partnership States*:

## *Oregon:*

**Domestic partnership law with rights identical to marriage enacted:** May 9, 2007

**Injunction against enforcement:** September of 2008 (A group of voters petitioned to overturn the statute on the state ballot, but were short by about 100 signatures; the group challenged the secretary of state's signature verification policy in court; the court enjoined enforcement until the issue was resolved.)

**Domestic partnership law takes effect:** February 1, 2008

**Domestic partnerships performed:** February 4, 2008

## *Nevada:*

**Domestic partnership law with rights nearly identical to marriage enacted (over governor's veto):** May 31, 2009 (Slightly different from marriage because domestic partners must share a common residence, must be at least eighteen, rather than sixteen for marriage, and health insurance companies do not have to extend benefits to partners.)

**Domestic partnerships performed:** October 1, 2009

## *Wisconsin:*

**Limited domestic partnership law enacted:** June 29, 2009 (estate, family medical leave, hospital visitation)

**Domestic partnerships performed:** August 3, 2009

---

* Listed chronologically by date civil union or domestic partnership (DPs) with rights identical to marriage laws were enacted

## *Illinois:*

**Civil unions law enacted:** January 31, 2011 (same-sex and different-sex couples)

**Civil unions performed:** June 1, 2011

## *Hawaii:*

**Civil unions law enacted:** February 23, 2011

**Civil unions performed:** January 1, 2012

## *Colorado:*

**Very limited "designated beneficiary agreement" law enacted:** April 9, 2009 (funeral arrangements, death benefits, and inheriting property without a will)

**Designated beneficiary agreement law takes effect:** July 1, 2009

**Civil unions law enacted:** March 21, 2013

**Civil unions performed:** May 1, 2013

Used with permission from GLAD, Boston, Massachusetts (www.glad.org).

# Endnotes

## Preface

1. *United States v. Windsor*, 133 S. Ct. 2675 (2013)

2. Kim Palmer, "Ohio must recognize marriage of same-sex couple, federal court rules," Reuters, September 3, 2013.

   http://www.reuters.com/article/2013/09/04/us-usa-ohio-gayrights-idUSBRE98301Q20130904

3. Freedom to Marry, States.

   http://www.freedomtomarry.org/states/

## Introduction

1. Jennifer Hoyt Cummings, "How to live up to your LGBT marketing," Reuters, June 8, 2013.

   http://www.reuters.com/article/2013/06/28/us-lgbt-wealthmanagement-idUSBRE95R0JW20130628

2. Maryland Same-Sex Civil Marriage Referendum, Question 6 (2012),

   Maine Same-Sex Marriage Question, Question 1 (2012),

   Washington Same-Sex Marriage Veto Referendum, Referendum 74 (2012)

   Minnesota Same-Sex Marriage Amendment, Amendment 1 (2012), which would have banned gay marriage in the state with a constitutional amendment, was rejected.

3. Jackie Calmes & Peter Baker, "Obama Says Same-Sex Marriage Should Be Legal," New York Times, May 9, 2012. http://www.nytimes.com/2012/05/10/us/politics/obama-says-same-sex-marriage-should-be-legal.html?pagewanted=all_r=0 US

Republican hopeful Romney rejects same-sex marriage, BBC, May 12, 2012. http://www.bbc.co.uk/news/18046282

4. Don't Ask, Don't Tell Repeal Act of 2010, H.R. 2965, 111th Cong. (2010).

5. *United States v. Windsor*, 133 S. Ct. 2675 (2013)

6. *Hollingsworth v. Perry*, 133 S. Ct. 2652 (2013)

7. Kevin Mumford, expert on the histories of race relations and sexuality, University of Illinois at Urbana-Champaign, July 2, 2013. http://illinois.edu/lb/article/72/75283

8. *Garden State Equality, et. al. v. Paula Dow, et. al.*, N.J. Docket No. 073328 (Op. on Mot. for Stay Pending Appeal, Oct. 18, 2013). http://www.judiciary.state.nj.us/samesex/Supreme%20Court%20Opinion%20on%20Stay%20Motion.pdf

9. *Garden State Equality v. Paula Dow, et al*, Superior Court of NJ, Docket no. L-1729-11, Sept. 27, 2013

10. *Goodridge v. Dept. of Public Health*, 798 N.E.2d 941 (Mass. 2003)

11. Mitt Romney, "One Man, One Woman: A Citizen's Guide to Protecting Marriage," Wall Street Journal, February 5, 2004.

12. The Washington Post, "Transcript: Third Presidential Debate," October 13, 2004.

http://www.washingtonpost.com/wp-srv/politics/debatereferee/debate_1013.html

13. Jonathan Rauch, "Gay Marriage: Why It Is Good for Gays, Good for Straights, and Good for America" (2004); and E.J. Graff, "What is Marriage For?: The Strange Social History of Our Most Intimate Institution," (2004).

14. Defense of Marriage Act, Public Law No. 104-199, September 21, 1996.

# Chapter 1

1. Much of the material in this chapter is from E.J. Graff's terrific work titled, What is Marriage For? (Beacon Press, 2004).

2. Aurelius Augustin, Bishop of Hippo, On Marriage and Concupiscence.

   http://www.newadvent.org/fathers/1507.htm

3. *Loving v. Virginia*, 388 U.S. 1 (1967)

4. *Lawrence v. Texas*, 539 U.S. 558 (2003)

# Chapter 2

1. See, e.g. Albert Ellis, "Homosexuality: Its Cause and Cures" (1965); or Lother B. Kalinowsky, "Shock Treatments, Psychosurgery, and Other Somatic Treatments in Psychiatry," (1952).

2. See *Lawrence v. Texas*, 539 U.S. 558 (2003)

3. Ronald Bayer, "Homosexuality and American Psychiatry: The politics of Diagnosis," (1987).

4. Homosexuality, Stanford Encyclopedia of Philosophy, February 11, 2011.

   http://plato.stanford.edu/entries/homosexuality/#His

5. There are many reports about this incident. My favorite headline was from The New York Daily News: "Homo Nest Raided: Queen Bees are Stinging Mad," by J. Lisker, July 6, 1969.

6. Scott Bravmann, Queer Fictions of the Past: History, Culture and Difference, (1997).

7. *Collamore v. Learned*, 171 Mass. 96 (Mass. 1898) where Justice Holmes found that adult adoption was "perfectly proper" to secure inheritance rights.

8. Susan Donaldson James, "Gay Man Adopts His Partner to Avoid Inheritance Tax," June 8, 2013, ABC News.

   http://abcnews.go.com/Health/gay-man-adopts-partner-avoid-inheritance-tax/story?id=19512067

9. *In re Adoption of Robert Paul P.*, 471 N.E.2d 424 (N.Y. 1984).

10. Human Rights Campaign, Domestic Partner Benefit Eligibility: Defining Domestic Partners and Dependents.

    http://www.hrc.org/resources/entry/domestic-partner-benefit-eligibility-defining-domestic-partners-and-depende

11. EqualityMaine, Marriage, Civil Unions and Domestic Partnerships: A Comparison.

    http://equalitymaine.org/marriage-civil-unions-and-domestic-partnerships-comparison

12. Report of Government Accounting Office GAO-04-353R, January 23, 2004, Washington, D.C.

13. Nancy J. Knauer, "Gay and Lesbian Elders History, Law, and Identity Politics in the United States," (2011).

14. *Langbehn v. Public Health Trust of Miami-Dade*, 661 F. Supp 2d 1326, (S.D. Fla. 2009)

15. Tara Parker-Pope, "Kept from a Dying Partner's Bedside," New York Times, May 18, 2009.

    http://www.nytimes.com/2009/05/19/health/19well.html

16. Lambda Legal, Flaningan v. University of Maryland Hospital System.

    http://www.lambdalegal.org/in-court/cases/flanigan-v-university-of-maryland

17. M. Dubin, "Dispute Involving Headstone Epitaph Now a Federal Case: The Deceased's Parents And Gay Partner Are At Odds Over Her Wishes," Philadelphia Inquirer, June 26, 1997.

    http://articles.philly.com/1997-06-26/living/25525970_1_headstone-gay-rights-tombstones

    C.N. Ginanni, The Legal Intelligencer, September 8, 1997.

18. Lydia Saad, "U.S. Acceptance of Gay/Lesbian Relations Is the New Normal," Gallup May 14, 2012.

    http://www.gallup.com/poll/154634/acceptance-gay-lesbian-relations-new-normal.aspx

19. http://www.pewsocialtrends.org/2013/06/13/a-survey-of-lgbt-americans/5/#chapter-4-marriage-and-parenting

20. *Ibid.*

21. Chris Cillizza, "Why support for gay marriage has risen so quickly," The Washington Post, March 19, 2013.

    http://www.washingtonpost.com/blogs/the-fix/wp/2013/03/19/why-support-for-gay-marriage-has-risen-so-quickly/

## Chapter 3

1.  *Baker v. Nelson*, 191 N.W.2nd 185 (Minn. 1971); cert. denied; See also, *Jones, et al. v. Hallahan*, 501 S.W.2nd 588 (Ken. 1973) where a Kentucky Court of Appeals denied a lesbian couple the right to marry. That couple had made claims under other constitutional grounds, including the right to association and free exercise of religion; and see *Singer v. Hara*, 522 P.2d 1187 (Wash. 1974) denying a gay couple's right to marry by a Washington state appellate court on a variety of grounds.

2.  *Baehr v. Lewin*, 852 P.2d 44 (Haw. 1993), as clarified upon reconsideration (May 27, 1993).

3.  Jeffrey Schmalz, "In Hawaii, Step Toward Legalized Gay Marriage," New York Times, May 7, 1993.

    http://www.nytimes.com/1993/05/07/us/in-hawaii-step-toward-legalized-gay-marriage.html

4.  Bill Clinton, "It's Time to Overturn DOMA," Washington Post, March 7, 2013.

    http://articles.washingtonpost.com/2013-03-07/opinions/37528448_1_doma-defense-of-marriage-act-marriage-equality

5.  H.R. Rep. No. 104-664 (1996)

6.  Defense of Marriage Act, H.R. 3396 (104th)

7.  *Baker v. Vermont*, 744 A.2nd 864 (1999)

8.  "Governor of Vermont Signs Gay Union Law," New York Times, April 27, 2000.

9. Cary Goldberg, "Quiet Anniversary for Civil Unions," New York Times, July 31, 2001.

10. Mary L. Bonauto, Esq., "Goodridge in Context," Harvard Civil Rights-Civil Liberties Review (Winter 2005).

11. *Goodridge v. Dept. of Public Health*, 798 N.E.2d 941 (Mass. 2003)

12. *Brown v. Board of Education*, 347 U.S. 483 (1954)

13. Dan Ring, "8,100 gay, lesbian couples marry after 2004 decision." Springfield Republican (May 17, 2006), David Filipov, "5 years later, views shift subtly on gay marriage," Boston Globe, (November 17, 2008).

14. Carl Bialik, "For Gays, Breaking Up Is Hard to Do—or Measure." The Wall Street Journal, May 13, 2013.

15. Michael J. Klarman, "How Same-Sex Marriage Came to Be: On Activism, Litigation, and Social Change in America," Harvard Law School, (2013).

    http://www.law.harvard.edu/news/spotlight/civil-rights/klarman-how-same-sex-marriage-came-to-be.html

16. David Cole, "Getting Nearer and Nearer," The New York Review of Books, January 10, 2013.

    www.nybooks.com/articles/archives/2013/jan/10/getting-nearer-and-nearer/?pagination=false

17. Adam Gabbatt, "Edith Windsor and Thea Spyer: A love affair that just kept on and on and on," The Guardian, June 26, 2013.

    http://www.theguardian.com/world/2013/jun/26/edith-windsor-thea-spyer-doma.

18. Ibid.

19. Greg Botelho, "Victory for lesbian, years after her longtime partner's death," CNN, June 26, 2013.

20. *Sevcik v. Sandoval*, Dist. Court, D. Nevada 2012; Jackson v. Abercrombie, 884 F. Supp. 2d 1065

    Lambda Legal, Sevcik v. Sandoval.

    http://www.lambdalegal.org/in-court/cases/sevcik-v-sandoval

# Chapter 4

1. Annie Lowry, "Gay Marriages Get Recognition From the I.R.S.," New York Times, August 30, 2013.

   http://www.nytimes.com/2013/08/30/us/politics/irs-to-recognize-all-gay-marriages-regardless-of-state.html

2. Tara Siegel Bernard, "Gay and Married Couples in New Land of Taxation," New York Times, August 31, 2013.

   http://www.nytimes.com/2013/08/31/your-money/gay-marrieds-enter-new-land-of-federal-taxation.html?pagewanted=all

3. TurboTax, "Married Filing Jointly vs. Married Filing Separately," August 30, 2013.

   https://turbotax.intuit.com/support/iq/Filing-Status/Married-Filing-Jointly-vs--Married-Filing-Separately/GEN83639.html

   442 U.S.C. § 416(h)(1)(A)(ii)

4. Human Rights Campaign, "After DOMA: What it Means for You." http://www.hrc.org/files/assets/resources/Post-DOMA_FSS_Social-Security_v3.pdf

5. Ibid.

6. See, e.g. Barbara J. Cox, "Same-Sex Marriage and Choice of Law: If We Marry in Hawaii, Are We Still Married When We Return Home?" 1994 Wis. L. Rev. (1994); Joanna L. Grossman, "Resurrecting Comity: Revisiting the Problem of Non-Uniform Marriage Laws," 84 Or.L.Rev. 433 (2005) and Andrew Koppelman, "Interstate Recognition of Same-Sex Marriages and Civil Unions: A Handbook for Judges," 153 U.Pa.L.Rev. 2143 (2005)

7. DOL Technical Release 2013-04, September 18, 2013

8. "Retirement benefits no longer at risk for same-sex couples," Investment News, September 19, 2013.

   http://www.investmentnews.com/article/20130919/FREE/130919866#

9. Internal Revenue Service Revenue Ruling 2013-17

10. DOL Technical Release 2013-04, September 18, 2013

11. *Cozen O'Connor, P.C. v. Tobits, et al.*,
    Civil Action No. 11-0045, U.S. District Court, E.D. Pennsylvania.

12. Public Law 111 - 148 - Patient Protection and Affordable Care Act

13. E-mail from George Thomson of the Proctor Insurance Group (www.proctorgroup.com), August 9, 2013.

14. A. Herdy, St. Peter Times, August 29, 2001.

15. United States Office of Personnel Management Historical Federal Workforce Tables Total Government Employment Since 1962

    https://www.opm.gov/policy-data-oversight/data-analysis-documentation/federal-employment-reports/historical-tables/total-government-employment-since-1962/

16. United States Office of Personnel Management, Benefits Administration Letter 13-203, Coverage of Same-Sex Spouses.

    http://www.opm.gov/retirement-services/publications-forms/benefits-administration-letters/2013/13-203.pdf

17. Fed. Reg. 2013-22898

18. Bill Briggs and Jim Miklaszewski, "Outgoing DOD Boss Panetta Extends Some Benefits to Same-Sex Spouses, Partners of Gay Troops," NBC News, February 11, 2013.

    http://usnews.nbcnews.com/_news/2013/02/11/16927063-outgoing-dod-boss-panetta-extends-some-benefits-to-same-sex-spouses-partners-of-gay-troops?lite

19. United States Department of Defense, "DOD Announces Same-Sex Spouse Benefits," News Release Number 581-13, August 14, 2013.

    http://www.defense.gov/releases/release.aspx?releaseid=16203

20. United States Department of Justice, "Attorney General Holder Announces Move to Extend Veterans Benefits to Same-Sex Married Couples," September 4, 2013.

    http://www.justice.gov/opa/pr/2013/September/13-ag-991.html

21. Steve Rothaus, "Fort Lauderdale Gay Married Binational Couple First Recognized for Green Card," Miami Herald, June 30, 2013.

http://www.miamiherald.com/2013/06/30/3478678/fort-lauderdale-gay-married-binational.html

22. Julia Preston, "Gay Married Man in Florida Is Approved for Green Card," New York Times, July 1, 2013.

http://www.nytimes.com/2013/07/01/us/gay-married-man-in-florida-is-approved-for-green-card.html

23. Blake Ellis, "Nursing Home Costs Top $80,000 a Year," CNN Money, April 9, 2013.

http://money.cnn.com/2013/04/09/retirement/nursing-home-costs/index.html

24. Timothy Jost, "Implementing Health Reform: IRS Announcement On Same-Sex Marriages And Navigator Manual," Health Affairs Blog, August 31, 2013. http://healthaffairs.org/blog/2013/08/31/implementing-health-reform-irs-announcement-on-same-sex-marriages/

25. 26 U.S.C. Ch. 14

26. Scott E. Squillace, "GRITs for Gays and Other Unique Planning Opportunities for Same-Sex Couples," Practical Estate Planning Journal.

http://squillace-law.com/Portals/191865/docs/CCH_Practical.pdf

27. Rachel S., "How the Supreme Court's DOMA Ruling Impacts Student Loans," Tuition.io, July 23, 2013.

http://www.tuition.io/blog/2013/07/how-the-supreme-courts-doma-ruling-impacts-student-loans/

28. Scott E. Squillace, "College Financial Aid Disclosure for Families Headed by Same-Sex Couples"

http://squillace-law.com/Portals/191865/docs/College_Financial_Aid_for_Students_of_LGBT_Families.pdf

29. For more information on this benefit see: http://www.ssa.gov/pgm/ssi.htm

## Chapter 5

1.  NOLO, "Privileged Information at Trial: Spousal Privileges for Same-Sex Couples."

    http://www.nolo.com/legal-encyclopedia/privileged-information-trial-spousal-privileges-same-sex-couples.html

2.  Tim Ghianni, "Kentucky Gay Couple Seeks Spousal Privilege Protection In Murder Trial," Huffington Post, August 11, 2013. http://www.huffingtonpost.com/2013/08/11/kentucky-gay-couple-murder-trial-_n_3739212.html

3.  IRC §121

4.  S.B. 651, Section amending Family Code section 2320 (effective January 1, 2012).

5.  Lizzie Crocker, "The Gay Divorce Trap: When Same-Sex Marriage Goes Wrong," The Daily Beast, September 30, 2013.

6.  Internal Revenue Service, Rev. Rule 2013-17.

7.  *Elia-Warnken v. Elia*, 463 Mass. 29 (2012)

8.  Senate Bill 815 Employment Non-Discrimination Act of 2013

    Timothy R. Homan, "A Bill to End Bias Against Gay Workers," Business Week, September 19, 2013.

    http://www.businessweek.com/articles/2013-09-19/the-employment-non-discrimination-act-seeks-to-protect-gay-workers

9.  The Boston Foundation, Charitable Gift Annuities.

    http://www.tbf.org/giving/give-later/charitable-gift-annuities

10. Internal Revenue Service, Letter Ruling 9547004, August 9, 1995.

## Chapter 6

1.  http://www.hrc.org/blog/entry/memo-oregon-to-legally-recognize-out-of-state-same-sex-marriages

2.  See e.g. Barbara J. Cox, "Using Incidents of Marriage Analysis When Considering Interstate Recognition of Same-Sex Couples'

Marriages, Civil Unions and Domestic Partnerships," 13 Widener L. J. 699 (2004)

3. Phred Dvorak, "Why Just One Wedding Isn't Enough for Some Gay Couples," Wall Street Journal, Oct 30, 2008.

   http://online.wsj.com/article/SB122531715603381673.html

4. U.S. Citizenship and Immigration Services, "Gay Marriage."

   http://www.uscis.gov/portal/site/uscis/menuitem. eb1d4c2a3e5b9ac89243c6a7543f6d1a/?vgnextoid= 2543215c310af310VgnVCM100000082ca60aRCRDvgnextchannel= 2543215c310af310VgnVCM100000082ca60aRCRD

5. United States Office of Government Ethics, "Effect of the Supreme Court's Decision in *United States v. Windsor* on the Executive Branch Ethics Program."

   http://www.oge.gov/OGE-Advisories/Legal-Advisories/ LA-13-10--Effect-of-the-Supreme-Court-s-Decision-in-United-States- v--Windsor-on-the-Executive-Branch-Ethics-Program

6. Federal Election Commission, "Provisions Apply Equally to Same-Sex Spouses."

   http://www.fec.gov/pages/fecrecord/2013/september/ao2013-06. shtml

7. 42 USC § 416 (h)(1)(A)(ii)

8. Alexa Dragoumis, "After DOMA, Gay Couples Still Would Not Receive Many Federal Benefits," NBC News, July 7, 2013.

   http://firstread.nbcnews.com/_news/2013/07/01/19234205-after- doma-gay-couples-still-would-not-receive-many-federal-benefits?lite

9. United States Department of Labor, Fact Sheet #28F: "Qualifying Reasons for Leave under the Family and Medical Leave Act."

   www.dol.gov/whd/regs/compliance/whdfs28f.htm

10. 17 USC § 101

11. Pam Belluck, "Same-Sex Marriage Barrier Nears End in Massachusetts," New York Times, July 30, 2008.

http://www.nytimes.com/2008/07/30/us/30marriageweb.
html?_r=0;

see also: Chris Tomlinson, "Texas Guard Refuses to Process Same-Sex Benefits," ABC News, September 3, 2013.

http://abcnews.go.com/m/story?id=20145679

12. *Cozen O'Connor, P.C. v. Tobits, et al.*

Civil Action No. 11-0045, U.S. District Court, E.D. Pennsylvania.

13. *Christiansen v. Christiansen*, 253 P.3d 153 (Wyoming, 2011)

14. Associated Press, "D.C. Bill Allows Non-Resident Gays to Gain Divorce," New York Times, March 7, 2012.

http://www.nytimes.com/2012/03/07/us/dc-bill-allows-non-resident-gays-to-gain-divorce.html?_r=0

15. "Thanks to Romney, There's No 'Vegas of Gay Marriage,'" Advocate.com, February 10, 2012.

http://www.advocate.com/news/daily-news/2012/02/10/romney-i-saved-my-state-being-vegas-gay-marriage

16. *Martinez v. County of Monroe*, 50 A.D.3d 189 (N.Y. 2008)

*Port v. Cowan*, 44 A. 3d 970. (Md. 2012)

17. *Finstuen v. Crutcher*, 496 F.3d 1139 (10th Cir. 2007)

18. "Gay Dads Lose Appeal in Louisiana Birth Certificate Case," NOLA, April 12, 2011.

19. *Commonwealth v. Lane*, 113 Mass. 458 (1873)(Gray, C.J.)

20. See e.g. *State v. Ross*, 76 N.C. 242 (1877) where the North Carolina Supreme Court held a South Carolina inter-racial marriage as valid even though it was 'revolting to us' because of obligations of 'comity to Sister states.'; see also, *Bonds v. Foster*, 36 Tex. 68 (1871) and *Miller v. Lucks*, 36 So. 2d 140 (Miss. 1948).

21. Dan Barry, "Trading Vows in Montana, No Couple Required," New York Times, March 10, 2008.

http://www.nytimes.com/2008/03/10/us/10land.html?_r=0

22. "Gay Servicemembers Turn to Proxy Weddings for Federal Benefits," Huffington Post, September 3, 2013.

http://www.huffingtonpost.com/2013/09/03/gay-servicemembers-proxy-weddings_n_3857736.html

## Chapter 7

1. Marisa Allman, Sarah Greenan, Jai Penna, "Children and Same Sex Families: A Legal Handbook," Family Law, 2012.

   Joanna Thome, "Perceptions of Same-Sex Parent Families: The Roles of Traditional Gender-Role Attitudes and Anti-Gay Attitudes," UMI Dissertation Publishing, November 5, 2011.

   Shana Priwer, Cynthia Phillips, "Gay Parenting: Complete Guide for Same-sex Families," New Horizon Press, 2006.

2. American Radio Works, "Decision of the Century: Brown v. Board of Education," americanradioworks.publicradio.org/features/marshall/brown/html

3. American Association for Marriage and Family Therapy, "Same-Sex Parents and Their Children."

   http://www.aamft.org/imis15/content/consumer_updates/Same-sex_Parents_and_Their_Children.aspx

4. Daphne Lofquist, "Same-Sex Couple Households," United States Census Bureau, September 2011.

   http://www.census.gov/prod/2011pubs/acsbr10-03.pdf

5. William Meezan, Jonathan Rauch, "Gay Marriage, Same-Sex Parenting, and America's Children," Fall 2005.

   http://futureofchildren.org/futureofchildren/publications/journals/article/index.xml?journalid=37articleid=108

6. "FMLA Available to Married Same Sex Couple Residing in a State that Recognizes Same Sex Marriage But Not Available if the Same Couple Resides in a State that Does Not Recognize Same Sex Marriage," Protector Group Insurance, August 20, 2013.

http://pgcompliancecoach.wordpress.com/2013/08/20/dol-announces-fmla-same-sex-married-couple-guidance-fmla-available-to-married-same-sex-couple-residing-in-a-state-that-recognizes-same-sex-marriage-but-not-available-if-the-same-couple-resides-in-a/

United States Department of Labor, Family Medical Leave.http://www.dol.gov/dol/topic/benefits-leave/fmla.htm and see: United States Department of Labor, Fact Sheet #28F: "Qualifying Reasons for Leave under the Family and Medical Leave Act."

http://www.dol.gov/whd/regs/compliance/whdfs28f.htm

7.  Lydia Saad, "U.S. Acceptance of Gay/Lesbian Relationships Is the New Normal," Gallup Politics, May 12, 2012.

    http://www.gallup.com/poll/154634/acceptance-gay-lesbian-relations-new-normal.aspx

8   Rebecca Ruiz, "For Same-Sex Couples, End of DOMA Doesn't Mean Adoption Equality," Today News, July 20, 2013.

    http://www.today.com/news/same-sex-couples-end-doma-doesnt-mean-adoption-equality-6C10687368

9.  see e.g. *Johnson v. Calvert*, 851 P.2d 778 (Cal. 1993)

10. see e.g. K.M. v. E.G., 33 Cal. Rptr. 61 (2005)

11. Haya El Nasser, "Portland, Ore., Is Magnet for Gay Couples Wanting Babies," USA Today, May 11, 2013.

    http://www.usatoday.com/story/news/nation/2013/05/11/portland-gay-couples-babies/2139463/

12. Ibid.

13. Deborah H. Wald, Esq., "A legal Perspective on Gay Surrogacy," About.com Gay Life.

    http://gaylife.about.com/od/gayparentingadoption/a/gayparent.htm

14. "Adoptions by same-sex couples still on the rise," Adoptive Families.

    http://www.adoptivefamilies.com/articles.php?aid=2321/

15. Rebecca Ruiz, "For Same-Sex Couples, End of DOMA Doesn't Mean Adoption Equality," Today News, July 20, 2013.

http://www.today.com/news/same-sex-couples-end-doma-doesnt-mean-adoption-equality-6C10687368

16. "Adoptions by same-sex couples still on the rise," Adoptive Families.

    http://www.adoptivefamilies.com/articles.php?aid=2321/

17. Rebecca Ruiz, "For Same-Sex Couples, End of DOMA Doesn't Mean Adoption Equality," Today News, July 20, 2013.http://www.today.com/news/same-sex-couples-end-doma-doesnt-mean-adoption-equality-6C10687368

18. Teresa McMinn, "Same-Sex Marriage Can Cause Legal Issues," The York Daily Record, March 31, 2013.

    http://www.ydr.com/local/ci_22911961/same-sex-marriage-can-cause-legal-issues

19. Ibid.

## Chapter 8

1. Joan M. Burda, "Estate Planning for Same-sex Couples," (ABA 2nd ed. 2011).

2. For a more detailed discussion of these types of agreements, see Jared Laskin's work at www.palimony.com, "Why You Should Have a Cohabitation Agreement."

3. *In re Mullen*, 129 Ohio St.3d 417 (2011)

4. *See In re Bonfield*, 780 N.E.2d 241 (Ohio 2002)

## Chapter 9

1. Carol Kuruvilla, "Transgender Texas Widow Fighting for First Husband's Death Benefits," New York Daily News, September 20, 2013.

   http://www.nydailynews.com/news/national/transgender-texas-widow-fighting-husband-death-benefits-article-1.1463015

2. "Texas Judge Voids Transgender Widow's Marriage," Fox News, May 31, 2011.

http://www.foxnews.com/us/2011/05/31/texas-judge-voids-
transgender-widows-marriage/

3.  U.S. Social Security Administration, "Changing Numident Data for
    Reasons Other than Name Change."

    https://secure.ssa.gov/poms.nsf/lnx/0110212200

4.  *Kantaras v. Kantaras* 884 So.2d 155 (Fla. App. Ct., 2004)

5.  *Supra* Chapter 2, Note 13.

6.  Sam Skolnik, "Same-Sex Estate Rights Backed," Seattle Post
    Intelligencer, November 1, 2001.

    http://www.seattlepi.com/default/article/Same-sex-estate-rights-
    backed-1070576.php

7.  *Vasquez v. Hawthorne*, 33 P.3d 735 (Wash. 2001)

8.  *Supra* Chapter 2, Note 13.

# Chapter 10

1.  College for Financial Planning, Accredited Domestic Partnership
    Advisor or ADPA

    http://www.cffpinfo.com/adpa.html

2.  Marcum Group, "Same-Sex Marriage Unions by State."

    http://www.marcumllp.com/services/taxandbusiness/
    LGBT-non-traditional-fpg

# Chapter 11

1.  Benjamin Wiker, "'Gay Marriage' or Religious Freedom: You Can't
    Have Both," National Catholic Register, May 4, 2013.

    http://www.ncregister.com/site/article/gay-marriage-or-religious-
    freedom-you-cant-have-both

2.  *Sevcik v. Sandoval*, Dist. Court, D. Nevada 2012

    The complaint was filed in the Federal District of Nevada on
    behalf of eight couples denied marriage licenses, and the challenge

was based on an equal protection argument under the Fourteenth Amendment. On November 26, 2012, Chief Judge Robert Jones ruled against the plaintiff couples, holding that the equal protection argument was precluded by Baker. "The equal protection claim is the same in this case as it was in Baker, whether the equal protection clause prevents a state from refusing to permit same-sex marriages."

An appeal was filed on December 3 with the Ninth Circuit Court of Appeals, which will hear it on the same track as the Hawaii case, *Jackson v. Abercrombie*, 884 F. Supp. 2d 1065.

3. Robert Barnes, "Lawyers Olson and Boies want Virginia as same-sex marriage test case," The Washington Post, September 29, 2013.

4. *Palladino et al v. Corbett et al.*, Pennsylvania Eastern District Court, Case Number: 2:2013cv05641, Filed September 26, 2013.

5. John Culhane, "The Most Ingenious Attack on Gay Marriage Bans," Slate, October 2, 2013.

 http://www.slate.com/articles/news_and_politics/jurisprudence/2013/10/the_pennsylvania_lawsuit_with_the_best_chance_of_toppling_state_laws_against.html

6. Tom Goldstein, "The Untold Risks of the Supreme Court's Same-Sex Marriage Decisions," SCOTUSblog, September 19, 2013.

 http://www.scotusblog.com/2013/09/the-untold-risks-of-the-supreme-courts-same-sex-marriage-decisions/

7. *Garden State Equality v. Paula Dow, et al.*, Superior Court of NJ, Docket no. L-1729-11, Sept. 27, 2013

# Appendix A

1. *In re Marriage Cases*, 43 Cal.4th 757 (2008)

2. *Supra* Introduction, Note 8.

3. "Freedom to Marry, Why Marriage Matters to Native Americans."

 http://www.freedomtomarry.org/communities/entry/c/native-americans

4. William N. Eskridge, Jr. & Darren R. Spedale, Gay Marriage: for Better or for Worse?: What We've Learned from the Evidence, (2006).

   http://www.nytimes.com/2013/07/18/opinion/what-the-court-didnt-say.html

5. Eric Cameron, "Memo: Oregon to Legally Recognize Out-of-State Same-Sex Marriages," HRC Blog, October 17, 2013.

   http://www.hrc.org/blog/entry/memo-oregon-to-legally-recognize-out-of-state-same-sex-marriages

# Acknowledgments

A book like this takes a community of supportive people to make happen. This one was no exception. While many helped with thoughts, advice, comments, suggestions, proofreading and editing support, whatever mistakes are contained herein are mine alone.

At the risk of forgetting someone, I would like to thank the many people who helped make this happen and supported my work in a variety of ways, in no particular order of importance:

Those who sat with me in Maine during the summer of 2013 just after the Supreme Court cases were announced to review text and dig through research material, including Carolyn Wojtowicz; David Reichmann, Esq.; Marie Natoli, J.D., M.B.A., Ph.D.; and my sister, Marie Squillace, Ph.D. (the only other published author in our family).

Those fellow lawyers who provided insights on certain technical areas: Jake Geller (immigration); Mark Smith (divorce); John O'Donnell (bankruptcy); Joyce Kauffman (family law); Joan Burda (estate planning), and my own colleague, Carol Sneider Glick (elder law).

My trusted CPA friends also lent a helping hand, including the always helpful Laura Barooshian, her colleague, Erica Nadeau, and Steve Rodman.

Other professional advisors who work diligently to provide competent advice to those in our community, including Cathy Burgess at Morgan Stanley, John McGowen at Northern Trust and Penny Weeks at BNY Mellon.

Friends, clients and countrymen whose input and help was invaluable, including the Honorable Rosaria Salerno; Linda Moulton;

Jonathan Rauch; David R. Williams; Nadia Yassa, Esq., and the countless clients who have entrusted me with the honor of helping them wade through these murky waters to evaluate whether they should wed.

The very able advocates and leaders in our community who taught me a great deal about how to effectuate social change in our times, including my hero Mary Bonauto and the able team at GLAD, including long-time legal strategist Gary Busek; my friend and neighbor Maura Healy from the Massachusetts Attorney General's office, whose terrific legal work on the Commonwealth's case laid much ground work for the ultimate DOMA repeal; and all of the other advocates whom I've admired from afar that are affiliated with such terrific organizations as the ACLU, HRC, Lambda Legal, Freedom to Marry, and the many state marriage equality organizations, including the original, MassEquality, on whose board I had the pleasure of serving during the heat of the battle in Massachusetts.

The brave souls who put themselves out there as plaintiffs in every lawsuit brought, including my friends, Dean Hara, widower of the late (and first openly gay) member of Congress, Gerry Studds (D-Massachusetts); David Wilson and Ellen Wade, together with their spouses among the bravest original plaintiff couples in the *Goodridge* case, that in some respects started this all.

My ever-loyal team at our law firm, who not only helped keep our clients satisfied with the excellent work they do every day while I was a bit distracted with my book project, but who also assisted me in countless ways to bring this work to fruition: my law partner, Brian Olson, whose techie and graphic skills were almost as valuable as his thoughtful legal opinions and painful editorial suggestions about my grammar; my right hand man at the law firm, Brett Barthelmeh whose law school paper: "Queer Eye for the Wealthy Dead Guy" (Syracuse University College of Law, 2008) in some respects inspired me to get off the dime with this project; my own "Radar" (if you appreciate the M*A*S*H reference), John Hickey, who keeps all the trains running on time; Alison Wells and Ed Duhamel, both very capable law students, whom I expect will soon become terrific lawyers once they graduate from Suffolk Law School this spring; and David Hill, who is always willing to lend a helping hand.

The very able editorial and production, design and support team for getting a book like this done at Jenkins Group, Inc., including Jerrold Jenkins, Leah Nicholson, Rachel Jones, Yvonne Fetig Roehler, Kim Hornyak; designers Chris Rhodes and Brooke Camfield; Janice Karlovich, a very capable editor; and my own personal "book doctor," who more than once cured my ills, Marcia Layton Turner.

And, of course, last but never least, my incredibly smart (and handsome) husband, whose insights are often tough to hear and profoundly accurate. I cherish him and am so blessed to have his complete support in this work I do.

# About the Author

S cott E. Squillace is a leading legal authority on same-sex marriage and a nationally-recognized expert on life and estate planning matters specific to same-sex couples. The founder of Squillace & Associates, P.C., a boutique law firm in Boston's historic Back Bay, Squillace and his colleagues have advised hundreds of members of the LGBTQ community from across the country. He is a frequent lecturer on the topic of the legal, tax and financial planning concerns facing LGBTQ people, particularly same-sex couples.

Squillace's practice also includes estate, tax and philanthropic planning for high-net-worth individuals and traditional couples and families. He provides succession planning advice to privately held businesses, and corporate business law advice to closely held companies and their owners. Finally, he is often asked to serve as an independent trustee for trusts and estates of individuals and families.

Squillace has practiced law for more than twenty-six years, including living and working in Europe for ten years as a corporate lawyer. He began his legal career at Skadden Arps in Washington, D.C., and New York, and went overseas to assist with the opening of Skadden's Paris and Moscow offices in the early 1990s. While there, he was hired by Levi Strauss & Co. to be its Chief European Counsel. Upon returning to the U.S. in 2000, he assumed other senior level in-house corporate responsibilities before founding his own law firm in 2007.

Shortly after graduating from law school, Squillace began doing simple wills and health care documents on a *pro bono* basis for gay men diagnosed with HIV/AIDS. Believing it was among the most important and meaningful uses of his legal talents, he continued that work during twenty years of practicing corporate and international law.

Over the past decade, Squillace became actively involved in the equal marriage effort in Massachusetts. He served on the board of directors for MassEquality, the organization principally responsible for preserving the landmark equal marriage decision in Massachusetts. He is a certified Legacy Advisor of The Sunbridge Legacy Institute, a member of Wealth Counsel, a national group of estate planning attorneys who work collaboratively, and a member of the Purposeful Planning Institute, where he was a charter member. He is also a member of the International Society of Trust and Estate Practitioners.

He has served on the Boston Foundation's Professional Advisors Committee, and currently is co-chair of its Equality Fund, which is an endowment for the LGBT community in the greater Boston area. He is a member of the board of directors for the Boston Estate Planning Council, a member of the Finance and Investment Committee for the Episcopal Diocese of Massachusetts, and he also serves as a Corporator for Eastern Bank. He previously served on a number of non-profit boards, including the Fenway Community Health Center in Boston, where he chaired that board and the Stonewall Communities board. He is a member of the Massachusetts and National LGBT Bar Associations, Pride Planners, the Massachusetts Bar Association, and the Boston Bar Association.

Squillace has been named a "Super Lawyer" by *Boston Magazine* in 2013 and a "Five-Star Wealth Manager" each year since 2009 also by *Boston Magazine.* He has been quoted in the *New York Times, Wall Street Journal, Boston Globe, CNN Money, Bloomberg Business Week, Reuters, The Associated Press, National Law Journal,* and a variety of other press sources for his expertise on planning with same-sex couples.

Squillace is admitted to practice law in Massachusetts, New York, and Washington, D.C., as well as in Paris, France, as an Avocat. He is admitted to practice before the U.S. federal district court in the District of Columbia, the U.S. court of appeals for the D.C. Circuit and the United States Supreme Court. He holds a bachelor's degree from Fordham University in New York, and has studied at the Sorbonne University in Paris. He earned his J.D. from the Columbus School of Law at the Catholic University of America in Washington, D.C.

Squillace and his husband, Shawn Hartman, reside in Boston and South Berwick, Maine, with their two chocolate labs, Bernice and Zoie.

The author welcomes comments on this book and can be reached at the e-mail address below.

info@squillace-law.com

For more information about his law firm, visit:

www.squillace-law.com

# Index

Bold page numbers refer to glossary definitions. The letter n refers to notes on the page. Square brackets indicate text references to endnotes.